OUT OF ORDER
Young Adult Manual of Mental Illness and Recovery

BOOKS BY DALE CARLSON

Teen Fiction
Baby Needs Shoes
Call Me Amanda
Charlie the Hero
The Human Apes
The Mountain of Truth
Triple Boy

Teen Nonfiction

with KISHORE KHAIRNAR, M.SC.
Understanding Your Self

with HANNAH CARLSON, M.Ed., LPC
Addiction: The Brain Disease

Are You Human or What? Evolutionary Psychology
Cosmic Calendar: From the Big Bang to Your Consciousness
Girls Are Equal Too: The Teenage Girl's How-to-Survive Book
In and Out of Your Mind: Teen Science, Human Bites
Stop the Pain: Teen Meditations
TALK: Teen Art of Communication
The Teen Brain Book: Who and What Are You?
Where's Your Head?: Psychology for Teenagers
Who Said What? Philosophy Quotes for Teens

Adult Nonfiction
Confessions of a Brain-Impaired Writer
Stop the Pain: Adult Meditations

with HANNAH CARLSON, M.Ed., LPC
Living with Disabilities: 6-Volume
Basic Manuals for Friends of the Disabled

with IRENE RUTH
First Aid for Wildlife
Wildlife Care for Birds and Mammals:
7-Volume Basic Manuals Wildlife Rehabilitation

Bick Publishing House
YOUNG ADULT SELF-HELP & PSYCHOLOGY SERIES

UNDERSTAND YOUR SELF
Erin Anderson, Reviewer
ALA BOOKLIST

"This self-help manual can best be described as a **psychological survival guide** for the stage of life that can often be the most confusing and challenging: the teenage years. Carlson, a seasoned author of young adult nonfiction, argues that there is no one magic key that unlocks a happy existence and that there is no "self" that one must find, as many other books in this genre claim. She encourages readers to consider the commonalities between all humans and also the special sets of inherited circumstances that are not only unique to each person but inescapable. Relinquishing fear and self-doubt and strengthening relationships are common themes. Carlson incorporates many philosophies, including Christianity, Buddhism, postmodernist thought, and hard science. Illustrations by Nicklaus tease out the most meaningful quotes from the text to bring abstractions into an understandable and visual format. A good starting place for **practical and comprehensive tools in the counteracting of common teen problems, such as alienation and insecurity**."

UNDERSTAND YOUR SELF
Dodie Ownes, MLS, Teen Editor
SCHOOL LIBRARY JOURNAL

"I've been a fan of Dale Carlson's books for years, and her latest, *Understand Your Self*, leaves no doubt that **this author knows how to write for teens about what is going on in their lives and brains**. She deftly walks readers through the concepts of self, and self-awareness (which you'll discover are quite different!) and then proceeds to help teens relate these to their everyday actions at home, school, work, their relationships and communication. As the mother of a teenagers, I truly appreciate Carlson's observations of adult influences on their children's behaviors, expectations, and ability to relate to the world around them, making this manual not only **highly recommended for teens**, but also for those that care about them. Carol Nicklaus' delightfully simple illustrations punctuate the fine points with humor and affection. A bibliography, list of additional reading resources, web sites, and index are included. Appropriate for ages 12 and up, ***Understand Your Self* should be on all school and public library shelves**."

PRAISE FOR
Out of Order: Teen Manual for
Mental Illness and Recovery

"I think *Out of Order: Teen Manual for Mental Illness and Recovery* will be of great service to teenagers. I see it as a 'go-to' book for therapists and hospitals serving young adults, as well as for parents and teachers involved with troubled teens. The self-tests and mental health disorders dictionary are pure gold."

— Dr. Michael Bower, Ed. D., Psychotherapist

"I particularly like the way Dale Carlson has organized this book on teen mental illness and recovery, starting with the general explanation of teen mental illnesses, moving into more specific categories. *Out of Order* is full of anecdotes, lists of symptoms and signs, examples, definitions, and references to further information and treatment. I like the way Carlson describes how all people have many of these characteristics to some extent, so that young adults like myself do not feel so lost and crazy. Her personal knowledge of mental illness and her honesty set this book apart.

— Melissa Toni, 22, Young Adult Editor, Bick Publishing House

PRAISE FOR
Understand Your Self

"I would like to congratulate you for the book. The meticulous study of the formation of the self and its suffering, and the exercises given at the end of each chapter make *Understand Your Self* a practical manual for the understanding of oneself."

— Kishore Khairnar, M. Sc., Director, Krishnamurti Education Trust

"*Understand Your Self* examines the most elusive notion throughout the history of neuroscience: the human self…This manual shows us how to truly understand the structure of ourselves."

— Jason DeFrancesco, Yale New Haven Hospital

PRAISE FOR
Other Bick Publishing House Books

Addiction: The Brain Disease
"Addiction: The Brain Disease breaks down the stigma regarding
the nature of addiction. The raw truth regarding the physical, social,
emotional, and psychological aspects of addiction, as well as help and
recovery, are presented medically and through personal stories. This
book unlocks the door of hope to any suffering from the disease of
addiction to substances and/or behaviors. Carlson covers every base
from medical neuroscientific information to self-tests to solutions in
recovery."

— Jason DeFrancesco, Young Adult Editor, Yale-New Haven Medic

Cosmic Calendar: The Big Bang To Your Consciousness
"Overview of the origin of the universe...brain, body, genes, sex,
consciousness and intelligence...Carlson makes readers comfortable
with her probing tone...accurate and informative...good addition
science collections, good choice teen readers."

— Dodie Ownes, *School Library Journal*, goodreads.com

Are You Human or What?
"Humans tend to view themselves as separate from the rest of the
species and life on Earth, instead of connected. However, humans have
the ability to reprogram their thinking. Humanity will be responsible for
its own next psychological evolutionary step by the choices it makes.
The book...focuses on the brain as it relates to teen issues such as
loneliness, aggression, and sex."

— *School Library Journal*

"Carlson examines the new science of evolutionary psychology,
explaining the psychology of early man as it relates to human action
today. The objective is to show how we can evolve further into human
creatures who actually take and give joy in our lives...Evolutionary
aspects of the fear system, aggression and anger, evil, sex, lust and
human bonding are discussed, as well as how aspects of each emotion
might be changed to result in more humane behavior...The objective
of the book, to make teens recognize the source of their emotions and
that they can control and even change them, is admirable."

— *Voice of Youth Advocates (VOYA)*

Young Adult Manual of Mental Illness and Recovery

Mental Illnesses
Personality Disorders
Learning Problems
Intellectual Disabilities &
Treatment and Recovery

DALE CARLSON
Co-Author Dr. Michael Bower
Pictures by Carol Nicklaus

Bick Publishing House   2013   Branford, CT

Edited by Director Editorial Ann Maurer
Science Editor Hannah Carlson, M. Ed., LPC
Young Adult Editor Melissa Toni
Book Design by Jennifer A. Payne, Words by Jen
Cover Design by Greg Sammons

www.bickpubhouse.com

Library of Congress Cataloging-in-Publication Data

Carlson, Dale.
Out of order : young adult manual of mental illness and recovery : mental
illnesses, personality disorders, learning problems, intellectual disabilities,
treatment and recovery / Dale Carlson, coauthor Dr. Michael Bower ; pictures by
Carol Nicklaus.
     pages cm
  Includes bibliographical references and index.
  ISBN 978-1-884158-37-7 (alk. paper : alk. paper)
1. Adolescent psychopathology--Juvenile literature. 2. Youth--Mental health
services--Juvenile literature. 3. Adolescent psychiatry--Juvenile literature. I.
Bower, Michael. II. Title.
  RJ503.C393 2013
  616.8900835--dc23
                                    2013003328

AVAILABLE THROUGH:
• Distributor: BookMasters, Inc., AtlasBooks Distribution,
   Tel: (800) BookLog, Fax: (419) 281-6883
• Baker & Taylor Books
• Ingram Book Company
• Follett Library Resources, Tel: (800) 435-6170 Fax: (800) 852-5458
• Amazon.com

Or: Bick Publishing House
16 Marion Road
Branford, CT 06405
Tel and Fax: (203) 208-5253

Printed by McNaughton & Gunn, Inc. USA

ACKNOWLEDGMENTS

To Ann Maurer, for her constant
editorial guidance and perfect ear.

To Carol Nicklaus, for her award-winning art.

To Greg Sammons, for his awarded covers.

To Jen Payne, for her impeccable
taste in interior design.

To Hannah Carlson, Director of Dungarvin's Group Homes
for Adults with Mental Disabilities, for the astuteness of her
psychological insights and her diagnostic expertise.

To the courage of young people everywhere
who are willing to take responsibility
for themselves and toward the world.

CONTENTS

INTRODUCTION

Most Human Mental Disorders Start During Our Teens

Teens need to know about mental illness because most of the major mental disorders begin during adolescence—then carry over into adulthood. Teens need to understand their own emotional, behavioral, or developmental problems. They must learn the difference between passing moods due to the usual stresses of life, and the disabling mental and emotional pain of psychiatric illness.

Don't Just Stand There

Teens need to participate in all decisions about the identification of their symptoms, the diagnosis made, and the treatments available: the different therapies, psychiatric medications, support and maintenance to prevent relapse. *Because if teens do not take part in decisions about their own mental health, they are needlessly turning their wills and their lives over to the care of others!*

You Are Not Alone

All human brains are pretty much the same. This means we are all damaged to some extent and often wrong. So you are not alone. Mental health is only a question of degree, not difference. We are all on the same continuum. All people experience psychiatric symptoms like anxiety or grief or sadness from time to time. It's a question of how long the feelings last, and how, if, and whether they are disabling. A disability obstructs or interferes with living life, relating to others, meeting ordinary needs—just getting along in daily life.

Scientists say the human brain is the most complex thing they have yet discovered in the universe. So it's not surprising if something goes wrong or needs some professional tech support.

People with what psychologists call mental illness, such as psychoses or personality disorders, or addictions, or who have learning problems, developmental delays, or neurological tics—all are just like the rest of the human race. Every one of us occasionally experiences emotional imbalances, or has a brain wired wrongly or differently, or is addicted to something or someone. Sometimes these experiences pass, sometimes we need help in sorting ourselves out. Mental illnesses are a matter of faulty biochemistry. They can be due to inherited genes, our upbringing, our culture of violence. They can be due to personal experience, or to a physical accident. Mental illness is not a character weakness, a personality flaw, or a sign we are bad people. We all have brain faults. No one is born perfect; no one escapes some kind of trauma.

To Be Human Is to Suffer.

Also, we all suffer mentally, from our thoughts, from our feelings. Aren't you sometimes afraid of something that might happen or once happened to you? Aren't you sometimes lonely or angry, disturbed by desire for sex or money, or things other people have that you don't? It's hard to live a human life because our species' brains can imagine and therefore fear the future—or a repetition of past pain. We always seem to be afraid of not getting what we want, or losing what we have.

No one, teen or young adult, middle-aged or old, truly knows what they are doing, what we are all doing on this earth or to what purpose. If a madman had designed the human brain, he couldn't have done any better. Think about this, for instance: Humans invented nuclear warfare before we learned how to live together rationally and peacefully!

So—it isn't just you who doesn't have a clue how to live! Or goes a little crazy from to time. Sanity fluctuates for everyone.

People with diagnoses of mental disorders who are in treatment—medication, therapy, or support systems—may be no more or less sane than anyone else.

If you happen to be among those who have been diagnosed with a mental illness, you have not been given a new name. You are not a schizophrenic or a bipolar: you are just a person with schizophrenia or bipolar disorder on medication. No stigma is attached, any more than to a person with a broken leg who needs crutches to walk.

And let no one attach slang terms for mental illness to you. Your own name is still your own name. You are not nuts, mad, crazy, insane, retarded, screwy, or cracked. These are trash words like any other insult.

Out of Order is a manual and dictionary for teens and young adults of what can go wrong with the healthy functioning of your brain and what can be done about it. It's a book about what we know, and what we don't know, remembering always that scientists are still debating the causes of mental illness: genes, cultural environment, personal experience, evolutionary inheritance, and what part each plays.

Symptoms, possible causes, treatments, and relapse prevention are suggested for each mental illness, personality or mood disorder, developmental delay or disability, and for addiction.

Symptoms often overlap. Depression can present itself in many different mental illnesses, for instance. So misdiagnosis and the wrong treatment are possible. If you keep paying attention to yourself, and you seek a psychologist or psychiatrist who pays close attention to you, you'll receive a proper diagnosis and the best known treatment.

This book will help you to sort out your own symptoms, if like most people you are nervous about asking for help. It will guide you into asking for the help you need for treatment and recovery.

- Everyone experiences mental health problems from time to time.

- Mental health problems can be treated.

- Be responsible for paying attention to yourself, to your symptoms, for seeking help and treatment, and for your recovery. No one can take your pills, do your therapy, or live the rest of your life for you.

Section One

Chapter One

WHAT IS MENTAL ILLNESS?

What Is Sanity? Who Has It?

Definition of Mental Illness or Disorder

Mental disturbances have been classified by The American Psychiatric Association's textbook *Diagnostic and Statistical Manual of Mental Disorders*. This is lovingly called the *DSM* by those of us who need to handle it frequently. Are we all getting sicker? Or, as is understood by mental health professionals, we are still revising what we know about the human brain, its functioning and malfunctioning. In the meantime, people with mental disorders need a diagnosis, patients and doctors alike, to bill for third-party payments (someone besides *you* pays for your treatment), for which *DSM* is a reference.

According to *DSM*, *mental disorder* is defined as "Significant behavioral or psychological syndrome or pattern that occurs in an individual…with a significantly increased risk of suffering death, pain, disability, or an important loss of freedom."

In other words, mental suffering hurts. It turns off the lights in your world, so that everything seems dark or distorted. It's like living in a bad nightmare. Or getting lost without a map. The worst part is often the loneliness, the feeling of being different from other people. And the anxiety, the fear that the darkness will never end is relentless. With depression especially, the fear that it will never end is the worst horror of all.

Philosophers, religious people, scientists like Kishore Khairnar have told us that the major problem for the whole human race has never changed: that is, the problem of human suffering and how to to end it. But if on top of being an ordinary, suffering human, your brain is biochemically messed up, you feel and behave in even more self-destructive ways than more chemically balanced people. And these are feelings and behaviors over which you sometimes have little or no control in an effort to stop *your* pain.

Behaviors such as drug abuse, obsessive rituals, a constant compulsion for sex or romance, cutting yourself, over-eating, pulling out your hair, suicide attempts—none of these help stop the feelings for long. And giving in to emotions like depression, anxiety, and chronic anger doesn't help either.

To have mental illness without treatment is to live in a private, isolated hell.

Ask any of us who have lived there.

We Have All Experienced Mental Illness Symptoms

"No specific gene has yet been isolated that causes mental illnesses," says Dr. James Whitney Hicks in his book *50 Signs of Mental Illness*.

Scientists don't yet know exactly what causes mental illness, those flaws in brain chemistry and wiring that push someone across the line of acceptable feeling and behavior.

- If you have close relatives, especially parents, with mental illness, you have a higher likelihood of mental illness yourself.

- If you have been through great stress, the loss of your health, an arm or leg, your home and money, the loss of an important relationship like a parent, friend, or lover, traumatic personal attack, war, rape, such stressors can temporarily or permanently affect mental balance.

- Physical causes from brain injury or other physical changes in the brain may lead to temporary or permanent psychiatric symptoms.

The brain is far more complex than any other part of the body—so understanding its chemistry and functioning will take far longer.

But what Dr. Hicks says is that nearly one of every three of us experiences psychiatric symptoms each year. Anxiety, prolonged grief, depressive lows and manicky highs are part of most people's experience. It is when they last too long, when they disable us, when they distort our lives, that we must seek treatment. You may not need a doctor for a temporary sprain. But don't break a leg and try to walk on it without medical attention.

• •

WARNING: Because we all have some of these mental distur-
bances from time to time, be mindful of the danger as you read
this book of feeling or thinking you have every defect described.
States of being are not static. We all live with emotional and be-
havioral tides. We fluctuate naturally with the circumstances
of our lives. It is when troubling symptoms persist, dominate,
interfere with your functioning that you must question your-
self seriously. It is when moods and behaviors override what-
ever is going on, interfere with what is going on or with what
you want to do, that you must question your mental health.

*The issue is the **degree** to which you are ill. That is why it's impor-*
tant to recognize the signs of mental illness.

And if you feel you are in trouble psychologically, take responsibil-
ity for yourself by asking for help at home or in school. It's abso-
lutely more fun to blame home or school or anyone at all for what
ails you—but blaming won't help you get better. Getting help will
help you get better.

• •

What Is Sanity? Who Has It?

Philosophers and dictionaries define sanity as intelligence, as understanding and insight into what is actually going on in your life
and in the world. Sanity is perception without distortion either of
cultural prejudice or faulty brain cells, faulty wiring, faulty chemicals. The first part of sanity—understanding yourself— is up to you
alone. The second—your cultural flaws or brain miswiring—you
may need some help with.

Sanity, ultimately, is not how you are born, but how you live.

We are all born with primitive, unconscious parts of our brain that go back to our evolutionary animal beginnings. The oldest, back part of our brain, inherited from the dinosaurs, keeps us breathing, regulates us mechanically without our conscious effort. The middle part of our brain we share with all animal life. It It is the seat of the emotions that signal flight or fight, fear and anger, our survival modes.

Then there is the human mantle that covers the original two parts of our brain, the cortex. Consciousness, thinking, and judgment are a few of its functions. These highly complex human functions are easily thrown into confusion not only by the dangers of life but our own primitive brains overriding rationality. The human mantle cloaking the two primitive parts of our brain did *not replace* the older real estate. It only built on top of the still-functioning older parts.

It's not always evolution and genes.

The violent society human brains have created through our ancient animal fears of insecurity and danger, has frightened and crazed us all to some extent. War, rape, murder, crowd shootings, and the constant reminder of these violences in movies, video games, and nightly news broadcasts further excites and electrifies our fears. So if, on top of that, due to genes or accident you have faulty wiring or chemical imbalances in your brain, the storms caused by desires and fears can make living a sane and balanced life nearly impossible.

Parents, school, culture, society, physical environment or trauma, emotional or financial poverty may also share the blame for the possibly genetic expression of your mental illness.

As a person diagnosed and living with bipolar disorder and in recovery for addiction and alcoholism myself, I have to avoid getting high on the adrenaline rush caused by stress. I pay for the emotional highs with a stretch of those gray, deathly empty days of depression the mentally ill know only too well. Along with my medication, the right food and exercise, I need a balanced life and stable relationships for sanity. Emotional roller-coasting, though I dearly love it, plunges me into bad stretches of emotional suffering.

Introduction to Mental Health Disorders

Some mental health disorders can be diagnosed in infancy or childhood, but most of the major mental disorders are diagnosed during the teen years and then carried over into adulthood.

The good news is that most mental disorders are treatable with medications and psychotherapy. The rest of the good news is that a mental health disorder does not have to affect the whole of your life. Many geniuses and great leaders from Mozart to Einstein, from Kings of Europe, Emperors of China, to presidents of the United States, have suffered from the psychiatric disturbances of mental disorders, and have nevertheless done important work. See the movie *A Beautiful Mind*, read the letters of the painter Van Gogh to his brother, check the Internet for the stories of the great and mentally ill. But remember that now, even the severe, psychotic mental disorders such as schizophrenia, the mood disorders of major depression and bipolar or manic-depressive illness, are now treatable with medications and therapy.

The loose definition of a mental disorder is, in the simplest terms, a group of behavioral or psychological symptoms or patterns that cause suffering or an inability to function well enough to meet life's needs. The *DSM*, the manual most often referred to for diagnosis of mental disorders, groups mental illnesses.

Psychotic Disorders

Psychotic disorders are characterized by (present with, as doctors say) delusions and hallucinations, often with no insight into their delusional nature. Disorganized thinking, speech, or behavior, or catatonic behavior are part of the clinical picture. Psychotic disorders interfere with the capacity to meet the ordinary demands of life. Schizophrenia, schizophreniform disorder, schizoaffective disorder, delusional disorder, substance-induced psychotic disorder are various forms of this disturbance. Medication and therapy are now available.

Mood Disorders

Depressive disorders and bipolar disorders are the major mood disorders listed in the *DSM*. Depressive disorders are characterized by weeks of depression and loss of interest or pleasure in life. Irritability, changes in appetite, weight, sleep, decreased activity and energy or agitation, difficulty thinking and concentrating, feelings of worthlessness and guilt, thoughts of suicide are major symptoms.

Bipolar disorders are characterized by periods of depression alternating with periods of mania. Mania may exhibit inflated self-esteem or grandiosity, decreased need for sleep, more and more-pressured talking, flighty ideas, excessive pleasure-seeking activities like sex, foolish spending sprees, extravagant plans, unstoppable energy, irritability, especially if thwarted. Manic episodes interfere with school, work, ordinary activities.

Anxiety Disorders

Specific disorders such as general anxiety disorder (fear of almost anything), obsessive-compulsive disorder, agoraphobia (fear of going or staying outside your safety zone), social anxiety disorder (increased now by social media and texting instead of personal contact), separation anxiety disorder, phobias, post-traumatic stress disorder—all these anxiety disorders are manageable with treatment.

Personality Disorders

A personality disorder is characterized by a distortion in the perception of the world and one's self, as well as one's patterns of behavior. A classic example of personality disorder is Paranoid Personality Disorder, characterized by beliefs that others can't be trusted, are out to do one harm. The reactive behavior can be disabling, destructive to relationships.

Other Disorders

Gender-identity disorders, eating disorders, sleep disorders, impulse-control disorders like kleptomania (shop-lifting) or hair-pulling, personality disorders like borderline personality disorder or anti-social personality disorder—all are treatable with medications and therapy.

Learning Disorders

Learning disorders are disorders in processing information. These are usually detected in early school years. They include reading disorders such as difficulty in recognizing letters and words, difficulty with reading left to right (dyslexia). There may also be writing disorders—difficulty with handwriting and spelling. There may be a mathematics disorder, spatial recognition problems. There can be coordination disorders, difficulties with walking, feeding, getting dressed, sports. Language disorders, hearing disorders, and other processing disorders are all helped with patience and therapy. Attention deficit hyperactivity disorder (ADHD, ADD), oppositional defiant disorder, and other behavioral disorders are all treatable now.

THE SUBSTANCES OF ABUSE

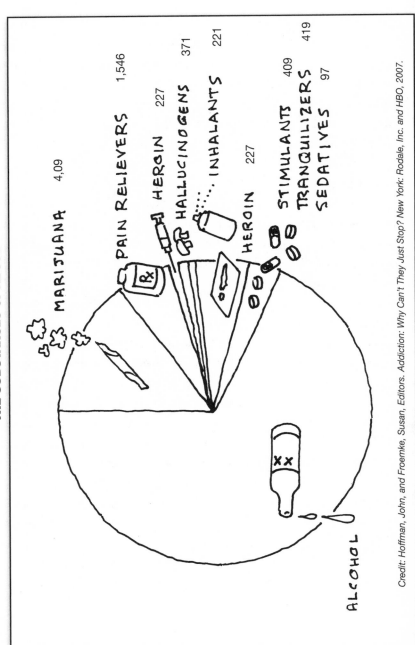

MARIJUANA 4,09

PAIN RELIEVERS 1,546

HEROIN 227

HALLUCINOGENS 371

INHALANTS 221

HEROIN 227

STIMULANTS 409

TRANQUILIZERS 419

SEDATIVES 97

ALCOHOL

Credit: Hoffman, John, and Froemke, Susan, Editors. Addiction: Why Can't They Just Stop? New York: Rodale, Inc. and HBO, 2007.

Intellectual Delay or Disorder

The development of mental and social functioning may be delayed or altered through genetic and/or environmental factors. Autism, Asperger's, other social interaction impairment, Down's syndrome, fragile X syndrome, viral infections, the use of alcohol and drugs during pregnancy, physical trauma, compromised oxygen supply, childhood infections of the brain, head injuries from falls, physical abuse, a deprived environment—there are many possible causes of learning delays, disabilities, partial or severe delay of mental development. Both genes and environment play a part.

Addiction: to Substances and Behaviors

Abuses of substances are common in adolescence. Alcohol, marijuana, cocaine, opioids, pain relievers, heroin, hallucinogens, inhalants, stimulants, tranquilizers, and sedatives, and there are always new club or party drugs, are all used and abused by teens. They activate the brain's pleasure pathways, and what started out as a temporary escape from the pain and confusion of the teen years, can become a mental and biophysical crippling addiction.

Addictions to eating behaviors such as anorexia or bulimia, sex and romance, pornography, shopping, video games, social media and the internet, gambling can all be arrested by prevention and recovery treatment, often with simultaneous psychotherapy and psychiatric meds that affect the serotonin and dopamine levels of the brain (the pleasure chemicals).

You may notice that a major symptom of addiction, in dependency of any kind, whether to a drug or an activity or another human being brings, along with the pleasure, the pain of withdrawal and so the ongoing desperate craving for the next fix. If joy is to be found, it turns out, it's to be found in freedom from addiction, not dependency. *(See Chapter 5 for more on addiction.)*

Many adults say one thing, think
another, and act out something else.

Suicide

Suicide is not usually listed as a mental illness or disorder. I have
listed it here because teen suicide has so increased that the psychological conditions of our society must be held accountable. Natural
evolution is about survival, staying alive and reproducing. It is not
about our young people killing themselves in a stifled cry for help.

According to the Annenberg Foundation's 2005 statistics, the
suicide rate among young people is now over double what it was
50 years ago. Reasons suggested were higher rates of depression
and substance use, lower family cohesion, and the greater availability of firearms, used in about 60% of suicides. Among U.S. high
school students, 9% attempt suicide each year.

We may have emerged from our caves and the hunter-gather-
er life ten thousand years ago. Our brains may have evolved and
matured enough to invent a universe of cyberspace and enough
sophisticated robotic warfare to kill off our entire species. But whatever part of the brain it takes to love one another, to connect with
one another and live in peace remains still undeveloped.

Many adults say one thing, think another, and act out something
else. We say killing is wrong, but we not only declare war, we send
our children to do the killing. We tell our young to be kind, to take
care of one another—and teach them to murder each other on the
playing field and later on in worldly ambition or war.

No wonder the more sensitive and intelligent of our children
and teens see through the adult world and lose their sanity But
suicide is a permanent solution to a temporary problem. Emotions
are always temporary because they change. They don't last forever.
Suicide stops the change process.

The help for this suicidal despair lies in talking about it, with each other, with friendly adults, in professional therapy. The help lies in understanding that your generation does not have to live the same way or according to the same values as previous generations have lived. **Live the story of your lives your own way.** This does not mean live irresponsibly. It means understanding the frightened human brain, and **doing no harm—to yourself or anyone else**. We may each live alone inside our own skins, as educator R.E. Mark Lee says. But we can learn to understand ourselves and each other. *And we can hold each other's hands instead of banging one another over the head like baby savages in a sandbox.*

Adolescence and Mental Illness

Our brains develop and change throughout our lives. Experiences, new information, a growing body—everything that happens to us, including our own thoughts, feelings, different behaviors, changes the brain's nerve cells and their electrical activity, the messages they send.

Adolescence, psychologists and other scientists generally agree, lies between the ages of 10 to 22. It can begin even earlier, and neuroscientists are now saying the brain doesn't complete its basic development until the age of 24. We further infantilize our young by keeping many of them in school, college, university, so as to manipulate kids into an increasingly complex society, long past the age of puberty and the flowering of their reproductive instincts. On top of this, we give them guns, cars, alcohol, drugs, and the right to vote before they reach mental maturation. Humans seem to have lost or forgotten the art and purpose of bringing up and educating their young to create and occupy a decent world for themselves and each other.

What is Adolescence, and Why Focus on the Mental Problems of Teens and Young Adults?

According to Doctors Dwight Evans and Martin Seligman in the Annenberg Foundation's book *Treating and Preventing Adolescent Mental Health Disorders*, adolescence is when most mental illnesses present their symptoms. At least one in five young people suffers from a current developmental, emotional, or behavioral problem.

Teens and young adults are entitled to get help to reach their potential as human beings. This involves the identification, treatment, and prevention of mental disorders.

It also involves the understanding that we still do not entirely understand the human brain. So young people also need to find out what we do know, what we don't know, and what we are doing research on to find out.

This Book's Contents:

● *Section One:* As listed in the Table of Contents, this section of ten chapters discusses the general definition of mental illness, descriptions of various kinds of mental disorders, treatments, and recovery

● *Section Two:* Self-Test Questions

● *Section Three:* A Mental Disorders Dictionary that describes:

   1. Symptoms

   2. Treatments: cognitive and behavioral talk therapies, psychotropic medications, prevention, recovery

3. Causes: what we think we know, what we don't yet know

4. Age of onset

5. Prognosis, or what will likely happen to you and your mental illness during the rest of your life both with and without treatment

● *Section Four:* Resources including hotlines, help and resources, organizations, websites

As you go through this book, you will discover that you may feel you have every mental disease, disorder, illness you read about. Don't take your own word for it. Consult a psychiatrist, a psychologist, a social worker, your own medical doctor, a therapist at school, or anyone in the mental health business.

Because mental illnesses are human conditions, most of us will recognize the conditions from our own experiences. Recognizing a condition or part of a condition does not mean that you have it.

One way or another, we're all looking for help.
You don't have to suffer alone.

STORY
RIDING THE WIND

"Morning terrors, black depressions, and ecstatic highs have raged inside me all my life. I have never been comfortable two minutes together since I was born. Even asleep, nightmares alternate with rapture in my eternal dreaming.

Sailboats respond to whatever wind blows out there on the water.

Manic-depressive, or bipolar, people like me whip about in response to inner winds that slow down or speed up according to our brain chemistry.

Teenagers, when I was young, were not diagnosed with bipolar illness. We were good or bad, outrageous or under control. Parents and teachers were the arbiters, not psychiatrists, psychologists, social workers, and counselors.

It took years before a psychiatrist diagnosed me. I was finally having what my grandmother would have called a nervous breakdown. My cycling was rapid. I went from manic states full of panic attacks, obsessive talking and behaviors, uncontrollable addictions to alcohol, lovers, and shopping, to periods of crippling depression when I could only sit at the dining table in my bathrobe doing jigsaw puzzles.

I was put in therapy sessions with a psychiatrist, on lithium and anti-depressants, and eventually told to go to Alcoholics Anonymous meetings.

By then I had been married and divorced twice. I had written a lot of books, and been published fifteen times, optioned a movie, supported two husbands, two young children, and assorted animals. I had traveled the world, lived in a rice paddy near an opium port in Japan, drunk my way into alcoholism and addicted myself to pills.

My Teens Could Have Been Predicted by My Childhood

Even when I was a little girl, my inner being had rhythms that danced or wept or froze, not in response to whether I was at a Christmas party or doing time out facing a corner wall, but only in response to biochemical changes in my own mood and energy swings. No one could cheer me when I was down. Nothing could make me sad when I was up.

In my life, my brain chemistry and the behaviors it dictated ruled.

This, of course, made my mother, teachers at school, counselors at camp, friends and enemies alike, think of me as entirely self-centered.

Myself, at least half a dozen presidents of the United States, Mozart, many great artists and leaders have suffered and gloried in mood-cycling bipolar disorder. So if you are diagnosed with this, you are in good company. We may upset other people, but we're in good company.

Ask me if I would change, and if I could, I would not. In my self-hate, I have always been prepared to endure the suffocating depressions. I would not exchange anything for the glory of the highs. It is, however, a hard way to live.

My Teen Years Went Something Like This

I woke up in the middle of a nervous breakdown every morning of my life. The terror at just having to face another day being me, of having to be with people, at just getting out of bed, at performing another day as if I belonged in the world as my friends did, was paralyzing. Let no one tell you the mentally ill lack courage and will power. To this day, even after years of talk/cognitive/behavioral therapy, psychiatric medication, and support groups, my morning hours are like pushing a heavy boulder up a steep mountain in the rain.

What's the alternative? Think about it.

If I can survive the morning with its panic and depression, and I'm not in one of my cyclic six-week depressions in spring and fall, the clouds lift by lunch. My mood lifts incrementally, until by evening I am cheerful. Then, at about the time everyone I know is ready for bed, I am ready to party. I never understood why my friends didn't want to go to a midnight movie, or hang out for a drink or a smoke or whatever.

My twice-a-year deep depressions in my teens, not yet diagnosed, therapized, or medicated, were alarming affairs. There are photographs of me then that would have set a werewolf's teeth on edge. I had been sent to a school outside of New York City proper for smart teens with 'problems', but even there I was in trouble pretty much all the time. I had developed character disorders, they're called now, to thrash my way out of the death-grip of depression. Oppositional behavior was the least of it, and one teacher after another said to my parents, "She's a born leader—if only she would lead them in the right direction." Or "She's so bright, why does she spend all her energy chasing boys?"

Silly questions. Making trouble gave me a spurt of adrenaline. Falling in love, especially with 'bad boys,' gave me spurts of adrenaline, dopamine, and norepinephrine that were the only antidotes I knew to lift me out of the bottomless pits of hell called deep depression. I was a love-and-romance addict by the time I was thirteen. I was an active alcoholic not many years thereafter. I have social disabilities (I don't read other people well), so I don't pick mates appropriately, hence all the breakups and later on divorces. In my race out from under the black clouds, I make all kinds of decisions about boys and men all kinds of badly. And, in my need for those spurts of my brain's pleasure chemicals, much too quickly.

I have been in and out of love with someone, or some country or atmosphere, or some book or movie or animal or friend, all my life, and with all my excessive energy, at great speed and with great intensity.

Thanks be to the Goddess, I have a quick brain and some talent as a writer. My mother never liked me much (I didn't share her hobbies—marriage, money, furniture). My fear of her, and her vocal and physical rejection of me has acted as a stressor all my life. It can to this day trigger quick cycling moods during the course of a day, when a relationship or my work goes badly. My father did like me, and encouraged me and the books I had already begun to write in my late teens. He once said to me, "Cultivate your brain—it will keep you company when your emotional life disappoints." I wonder how he knew? Genes, of course, I know now. This strange mental biochemistry is inherited. His support was a major gift to me, as it is for all of us with mental disorders, and his understanding that work, rather than people, would probably stabilize and sustain me.

Living with Bipolar Disorder Today
It took decades to discover that a combination of the antidepressant Prozac, meditation, walking for exercise and fresh air, a relationship with nature and connection to the universe, all worked better for me than my addictions to romance, alcohol, or anything else.

I had been creating tornadoes to counteract tornadoes—instead of just letting the winds die out by sitting still or behaving appropriately. The wreckage, once considerable, stopped.

A mind must be concerned with the workings of its own machinery, I've learned. The brain, the mind, is the machinery that drives your life. If your brain's perceptions of life and people, places, what happens to you, are all cockeyed, so is your life.

For some of us to manage accurate perceptions, it requires psychiatric medication for our peculiar brain chemistry, and rerouting behavior and therefore brain pathways, through talk therapy or support groups.

People like me, with untreated mood disorders, have a hard time of it. And being a human being is hard enough for anyone."

Chapter Two

IN OR OUT
OF ORDER

Who's Crazy?

This is not a term you'll hear professionals in the field of mental health use.

This is a term, however, you'll hear used by some of us accusing the rest of us for not doing things *their* way. Accusers include parents and their children, boyfriends and girlfriends, teachers and students, bosses and workers. In short, 'crazy' is used by all of us about the rest of us.

So, who's really crazy? We all are. Just to be human, to have a human brain, is upsetting. Think about it. Your brain contains over 4 billion years of evolutionary life information, 4.4 million years of human species information, and that impossible question: does your survival, our survival, depend on competition or cooperation?

It's only a matter of degree as to how upset your brain gets when it confronts the human condition we all share: living as a technologically advanced but psychologically confused person in this world.

As you read this chapter, you won't be able to help looking for signs of mental illness in yourself, for symptoms or patterns of behavior beyond the 'normal' range. Guess what. You'll find them. One of them, some of them, all of them.

The reason for that is because we all exhibit 'abnormal' patterns of behavior sometimes. The boy who is shy and withdrawn at a party is exhibiting the same form of behavior as the schizophrenic patient curled up against a hospital wall. The girl, all excited, whirling about, talking and laughing without taking a breath is as hyper as someone gripped in mania.

The difference is that relatively healthy people bounce back from a mood or stress, do not lose touch entirely with reality, and go on with their lives. It's a matter of degree and extent.

What Is Mental Health? What Is Mental Illness?

The simplest definition of a mentally healthy person is one whose psyche can cope with internal and external reality well enough to get through life without suffering too much to function.

Or causing so much suffering that other people can't function.

If you harm yourself, or you harm others, get help. Your psyche has to be reasonably enough well regulated so that you can behave yourself without handcuffs or straightjacket. Mastery, most of the time, over internal and external stress is the general meaning of mental health.

That doesn't mean you can't have fits once in a while or depressions or even experience the whole range of emotional and behavioral patterns from mayhem to times of quiet withdrawal. But if your thoughts and feelings don't drag you like runaway horses down blind alleys, and you manage to get through your classes and wash your face, not kick someone, or lift a wallet or decide to live in a closet, you're probably okay. Balance is the hallmark of a healthy mind.

Your Brain, or Frankenstein's?

Your brain, although more complex, is a physical organ like your heart or your stomach or your liver. The brain's job is to keep you alive.

Its nerve cells and electrical transmissions register experience and store memories so you remember to breathe, eat, not to touch fire a second time, and where you left your cell phone. Because the brain is a physical organ, it responds well to proper diet, exercise, sleep, healthy living, *and medication to balance chemistry.*

Nobody knows enough yet about the mind/brain to measure how much suffering is enough or too much, however. Or to make hard and fast definitions about mental illness. There are, of course, behavior patterns that make society tend to lock up some of its members. Criminals, psychotics, those with severe mental disabilities, people who behave too strangely, make the rest of us nervous, so we put them in prisons and mental hospitals. We put them away partly for our own sense of physical safety and theirs. They may not be safe on their own. But we also put them away because we identify with them to some degree. They make us uncomfortable because they are a threat to our own stability. Seeing them, we fear our own loss of control. It isn't always easy to be 'sane'. We don't want any reminders around us of damaged minds.

A Matter of Degree, Types of Behaviors, Signs and Symptoms

There are people who seem to be ordinary, yet cause a lot of pain to others and to themselves. These are people who do not take their clothes off in public, rob banks, push heroin, drive drunk, or create disturbances of any public kind. Yet they seem strange to us.

Some are so isolated and alone, they face one long, gray day after another, totally cut off from all human relationships. These sad, drifting people aren't bothering anybody, but they aren't functioning well either. Some are homeless. Some live alone in isolated rooms, unable to touch and be touched by other people.

There are people who are unkind, indifferent or abusive to their children, verbally cruel to other people, bully, disrespect, hate them. Psychically, they are just as sick as some of those we lock away.

Mental illness can't be defined solely by who is or isn't wearing a straight jacket. Or by who does or who doesn't try on suicide.

The Physical Brain Produces Feelings as Well as Thoughts

Feelings do not come wafting by out of the air any more than do thoughts. Feelings, or emotions, are produced by the physical biochemical brain. Human evolutionary emotional memory pathways plus your own personal experiences produce your feelings as well as your thoughts. The parts of the brain important in generating emotion are in the mid-brain, the limbic system, including the middle brain's amygdala. In adolescence, the emotion system is maturationally ahead of the judgment system. This means the emotions/feelings of fear, anxiety, guilt, dread, worthlessness, dread, irritability, anger, insecurity, desire—all transmit their chemical messages throughout the body without much benefit of the temporal lobes' tempered judgment. "Feelings drive us crazy as well as thoughts," as Dr. Michael Bower, psychotherapist, says. "And if you don't pay attention to them, sometimes even more."

The origin of feelings is the same as the origin of thoughts—your brain and its memory banks.

Fear of fire—or people—is based on the memory that fire burned you once, or people hurt your feelings.

Desire for sex, romance, or French fries, or more money or clothes or a better smartphone, is based on the memory of the pleasure you once got from them, and the temporary relief from life's sufferings that pleasure gave you before, and you want again. This is the origin of addiction, too, the need for escape from life's pain.

Loneliness, self-hate, rage, despair that anything will ever get better, these emotions are all the dark side of joy, self-approval, confidence, and especially the open-hearted love that makes life worth living. Most of us don't learn soon enough that understanding the ways of the self, letting the bad come and go without making it worse, works better than addiction to escape.

It's because the frontal lobes, the brain's seat of judgment, do not form completely until the mid-twenties, that teens and young adults are too often in the grip of their negative feelings, and lack the judgment to balance them, sort them, get help for what can be overwhelming. After all, this is the stage in life when you are asked to make the most important decisions, about a mate, a career or profession or job future—and all this without sufficiently formed brain cells.

All of which brings some of us to the edge of night. Where confusion and desperation wait to push us over into darkness.

Suicide

Suicide is the third leading cause of death among people between the ages of 15 and 24 in the United States. The risk increases from the teen years on into the early twenties by 50%. Females try it more often. Males succeed more often.

This may be because of method. Girls tend to overdose, a state from which rescue is more likely than the gunshot preferred by boys.

Suicidal Thoughts

According to survey data from the Centers for Disease Control and Prevention, one in six high school students has seriously thought about suicide. Call these hotlines if you're thinking about suicide:

- National Hopeline Network, 1-800-SUICIDE (784-2433)
- National Suicide Prevention Lifeline. 1-800-273-TALK (8255)

n her book *Monochrome Days* written for The Adolescent Mental Health Initiative, Cait Irwin lists some warning signs and risk factors for suicidal tendencies:

1. Hopelessness and worthlessness feelings and thoughts.

2. Withdrawal from family, friends, usual activities.

3. Continual boredom and inability to concentrate.

4. Letting schoolwork, appointments, dates, personal hygiene slide.

5. Alcohol and substance abuse, other mental illness.

6. Symptoms of depression (see Index) or other mental illness.

6. Obsessing over suicide plans and methods.

8. Family history of suicide, stigma over seeking help, lack of access to mental health care, past experience with abuse, addiction to danger, loss of key relationship.

Get help if you recognize these signs, any of them, and they are not going away.

And get help sooner rather than later. Suffering at all, and especially suffering by yourself, is no fun. *Talk*—to your parents if you can, to a sympathetic teacher or school counselor, a family doctor, at the very least to your friends. Talk to someone you both trust and who you know has information and experience to draw on. A psychiatrist or psychotherapist are the mental health providers you need.

Help

If a friend is troubled with thoughts of suicide, always take this seriously. Call the hotline numbers, call the parents, call the police (911), call *somebody*—and most important, *do not leave your friend alone.*

This goes for you, too. If suicidal thoughts or feelings plague you, *don't you be alone, either.* Find comfort, find company, find help. That much misery is hard to handle, hard to dismiss, hard to crawl out from under, on your own. Even if you understand intellectually that everything passes sooner or later, the thought is hard to hang onto in the middle of a bad depression because it just doesn't feel that way. Be a good friend to yourself—get help.

Helpful Language

- **Disorders:** Symptoms, Signs, and Syndromes, and Diagnoses

- **Symptom:** the complaint you bring to your doctor

- **Sign:** the abnormal finding by your doctor

- **Syndrome:** a collection of signs and symptoms that usually occur together in a disorder

- **Diagnosis:** the disorders grouped together and given a label for treatment purposes (for instance, manic episodes plus depressive episodes is diagnosed as manic-depressive illness or bipolar disorder)

Psychiatrists have classified a wide range of mental disturbances into specific disorders in the textbook *Diagnostic and Statistical Manual of Mental Disorders*, or *DSM*, says Dr. James Whitney Hicks, M.D., in his Yale University Press Health & Wellness book *50 Signs of Mental Illness*.

No mental disorder can be diagnosed exclusively based on lab tests. Experience and research are also necessary. So find yourself, or have an adult you trust find for you, an experienced and empathetic mental health therapist.

Who Needs Help?

Who is suffering badly enough to need help? Who is or is not functioning well enough with the realities of life, the pain, the joy, the difficulties? Who is abnormal, normal, whatever those words mean? Who doesn't need help and who does, and what kind?

Words are not the same as feelings or states of mind, but since we can't always touch and sense one another, words are what we've got to use to try to define what is going on inside all of us. Labels can't describe or help a whole human being. But we need them as a sort of general shorthand to describe general states of being.

Mental Illness

A lot of psychiatrists, psychologists, social workers, neuroscientists, and others in the mental health field protest each other's definitions about even using that term. They sometimes say 'mental disorder' or 'maladjustment'—which doesn't help much either. The term used is not really important. It just means a person can't manage—which may be as good a definition as any. The brain is unable to respond or adapt accurately to the real world.

So, if your brain feels sad, or if your life feels bad for too long, you may very well have a mental illness. But it may well be a disorder that can be adjusted if not cured. Not only with meds and talk therapy, but by learning to utilize your strengths to support and make up for your weaknesses.

STORY
ISLAND SUMMER DEPRESSION

"That summer on Nantucket Island when Dana was nineteen, the black, suffocating cloud of Dana's depression contaminated everything she saw, felt, or touched, distorted the meanings of what people said and did, the way mirrors distorted bodies in fun houses.

It was not her first depression. Dana had been through these sickening black moods before. Ever since she could remember, there had been stretches of time when the dark cloud that came out of nowhere turned off the sun in her inner world. The emotional darkness made her fearful, particularly of people. Dana felt the darkness was visible to others, like a physical deformity. She felt unfit for human company, exposed in all her worthlessness, her neediness, and shame. Worse, she felt poisonous, as if she contaminated other people.

Dana had forced herself to leave the safe mummy-wrap of her quilted bed, walked out of the guest cottage her parents had rented for the summer, and down the rocky path toward the ocean. She could see from behind her mental wall that all was brightness out there. The sun's shimmering heat warmed the sandy beach, the jetty's rocks, the grass blowing on the dunes, the sea shining with diamonds. But the sunlit warmth never touched her. The people under the bright beach umbrellas seemed far away, chattering in another world.

Dana did not need her parents or her younger sister to tell her that the sullen, angry look on her face would frighten the fishes, never mind the very boys they hoped she would meet to cheer her and reassure her mother they had a marketable daughter.

And Dana could not explain that the very boys her mother had in mind for her would plunge her deeper down into the black loneliness and despair.

It was only the *other* kind of boy, the wrong kind, even the dangerous kind, who seemed to exert a chemistry that lifted, that excited, as an antidote excites, her own.

Dana knew her darkness scared off ordinary boys. She knew it exhilarated a kindred dark spirit in boys like her, and together they got the bright lights going again.

Dana noticed a young man walking along the beach. She saw him approach the gathering of the summer people in front of the club house from the public beach jetty.

Something familiar quickened in her, a silvery spurt of adrenaline, a mixture of fear and excitement.

She knew the signs. She had felt the rush of adrenaline before, whenever a certain kind of boy came near, with a certain kind of swagger, a certain look in his eyes, an animal's grace, a lack of –of what? –a lack if socially acceptable values?

Dana's own values were not socially acceptable. She had never valued what society did: propriety, ambition, power, money, position, marriage and family.

She valued friendship, the looking directly through eyes into hearts, and, and the kind of instant intimacy she called love in its most naked form.

And so she excused herself from under the shadow of the family umbrella, to cool off beyond the white-capped waves, and then to drift with the moving tide farther down the beach.

They came together quietly, without a word. Until she began to tremble.

"Don't be afraid. I won't hurt you."

"It isn't you I'm afraid of."

"Then why are you trembling?"

"It's me, it's myself I'm afraid of, my own feelings."

His arms tightened around her, holding her close in muscled arms against a strong chest. He wore a T-shirt, shorts, a workman's boots.

"I'll take care of you," he whispered. "You won't get hurt."

For three weeks, this was so. For three weeks, Dana lived beyond the cloud.

And then he moved on, down the beach.

And Dana slipped back into hell.**"**

Chapter Three

THE DISORDERED BRAIN

Psychoses & Mood Disorders

A s developmental psychotherapist Hannah Carlson says in her book *The Courage to Lead: Mental Illnesses and Addictions*, "Mental illness is not fun, ever. To someone who has a mental illness, life can be a nightmare, often terrifying and bizarre, always a prison of isolation when the brain is unable to respond or adapt accurately to the real world."

Disorders and Diagnoses

Mental illnesses involve significant disorders of thinking, feeling, judgment, functioning and behavior that cause psychological suffering, disability, loss of freedom, even death. Diagnoses identify a person's distressed *feelings*; obsessive, irrational, and/or psychotic *thoughts*; compulsive, disruptive, socially unacceptable, possibly dangerous *behaviors*.

The **degree** of any of these is what determines whether or not someone needs hospitalization or out-patient treatment. We are all living on a spectrum of mental health, and on some days we are more or less mentally healthy than we are on other days.

Mental illness should be thought of and respected, diagnosed and treated, as a legitimate illness—the brain, after all, is just as physical as the rest of the body. And mental illnesses, like illnesses of the body are diagnosed according to their symptoms and grouped accordingly into those previously mentioned.

- Psychotic Disorders

- Mood Disorders

- Personality, Anxiety, and Behavioral Disorders

- Learning Disabilities

- Intellectual Disorders, Delays, or Disabilities

- Addictions: to Substances, to Behaviors, to Others, to Oneself

Mental Differences Are Not Necessarily Mental Diseases

As you read, note that there is a wide range of behaviors and feelings that are on a normal spectrum. Families and cultures differ, personalities differ, gender expectations differ, and what may be considered normal or acceptable in one group or person, may be certifiable in another. Behaviors in musicians, artists, writers, and teenagers may differ from those of business people, without being grounds for lockup. Male behavioral culture in war and football games would ground a female. Hallucinations valuable in a shaman will not do well in a math exam. Rage may express itself as aggression in one culture, depression in another.

We Are All on a Spectrum

Mental health or illness is also, as we've said, on a spectrum. This chapter will help you recognize your symptoms and communicate them to your physician, a trusted friend or parent or teacher. But just as a few good days don't mean you are mentally healthy, a few bad days don't make you a psychotic.

PSYCHOTIC DISORDERS

Definition

The word psychotic is generally used for disturbances that include a loss of contact with reality and the onset of hallucinations (experiences that are not real) and delusions (thinking that isn't based in reality). Schizophrenia is the most prominent of the psychotic disorders. Among addicts, Substance-Induced Delirium may also present with similar symptoms.

Symptoms

Schizophrenia is best described as a loss of contact with reality, an inability to tell the difference between what is imagined and what is real. Schizophrenia can be described as not being able to tell the difference between what people are experiencing and what is really happening to them. People with schizophrenia lose the ability to relate to reality, to people, or to work. They may have delusions, imagine they are scarred or ugly when they are not. They may have hallucinations, often auditory, and imagine they hear voices telling them to hurt themselves or other people.

People who have schizophrenia may have delusions that they are being stalked, delude themselves they are spies or aliens or bugs, hear voices, imagine they are Jesus or President of the United States or Miss America. Hallucinations can involve any of the other senses as well, sight, touch, taste, and smell.

Often the hallucinations and delusions are frightening, threatening, brutally critical of the person who is sick.

Children, teens, or adults with schizophrenia are subject to psychic storms of heightened symptoms, temper tantrums, unusual ritual body and facial movements and tics, self-torture. Spirits haunt them, imaginary phantoms, voices may tell them to kill themselves or other people. Families may live in fear of their own psychotic children, siblings live in fear of a sister or brother, just as those with paranoid schizophrenia live in fear of their own demons.

The *DSM* lists several types of schizophrenia, including the Paranoid Type (delusions and hallucinations of persecution and grandiosity), the Disorganized Type (disorganized speech, inappropriate emotions and behaviors), and Catatonic Types (emotionless, even motionless). Schizophrenia is a disorder that seriously interferes with the ability to meet the ordinary demands of life, even to physically taking care of. oneself.

Causes

The debate is ongoing as to whether genetic inheritance is affected by environment in the case of schizophrenia. Studies of adopted twins in different families indicate that biological factors are the strongest factor, but that environment is also a factor.

Treatments
For all these disorders there are medications. Some of the side-effects are hard to take: shaking; weight gain; cotton-head, emotional numbness. The great fear for people with schizophrenia is of complete withdrawal into their own worlds, becoming catatonic.

Age of Onset
Schizophrenia generally presents its symptoms in the late teens to the mid-thirties, though more and more onsets in childhood at ages 5 or 6 years old are being diagnosed and treated.

Course and Prognosis
Most studies according to the *DSM* indicate that the course of this mental illness is variable. Some people with schizophrenia, under appropriate care and treatment, will experience periodic remissions, whereas others remain chronically ill. Structural brain abnormalities in people with schizophrenia are still being studied, and medications and treatments are being improved all the time.

Other Psychotic Disorders
There are other types of psychotic disorders besides schizophrenia:

1. **Schizoaffective disorder:** schizophrenic symptoms with major mood disorder (depression or mania).

2. **Delusional disorder:** there are delusions that appear reasonable but are not true, like "my girlfriend is cheating on me," or "I have an undiagnosed cancer." The delusions are not weird, but they're not real.

3. **Shared psychotic disorder:** when two people in a close relationship share a delusion.

4. **Substance-induced psychotic disorder:** some drugs, medications, or toxins can produce hallucinations.

5. **Brief Psychotic Disorder:** sometimes hallucinations or delusions last longer than a day but are gone within a month or so, and normal functioning returns.

Diagnosis

Differential diagnosis can distinguish one from the other, so that appropriate treatment can be applied to each medical condition for the best outcome possible. Proper diagnosis is key to proper and appropriate treatment.

MOOD DISORDERS

Definition

Mood disorders such as major depression are not based on external, situational reasons for feeling really bad like death or divorce, or organic disorders. Nor are the manic episodes in manic-depression or bipolar disorder based on winning the lottery or the person of your dreams.

The mood disorders, depression and mania, are complex brain diseases with multiple causes: genetics, biochemistry, and environment all play a part. Both tend to run in fami-

lies, like heart disease or diabetes. And both depression and mania are linked to changes in brain chemistry that involve neurotransmitters, the chemicals that ferry messages between brain cells.

Brain wiring, even nerve cell functioning, may also affect brain mood and brain activity. Human brains are all more or less alike, just as mouse brains are all more or less alike. But too much or too little of cellular chemicals, cells that fire too fast or too slow, can cause genius or depression, artistic talent or mental disorders and other personality peculiarities.

MAJOR DEPRESSIVE DISORDER

Symptoms

- Down, sad, blue, often irritable mood for at least two weeks, with a loss of interest, energy, and pleasure in usually pleasurable activities.

- Changes in appetite, eating too much or too little, gaining or losing a lot of weight.

- Changes in sleeping habits, either unable to fall asleep easily and startling awake during the night, or sleeping too much and feeling half-drugged during the day.

- Changes in activity level, decreased energy and interest levels.

- Difficulty thinking, concentrating, making decisions.

- Feelings of hopelessness and worthlessness, that life is meaningless and not worth living, guilt and self-hate, personal responsibility over things beyond control from parental drinking to world hunger to one's own depression.

- Suicidal thoughts and plans.

- Presence of second disorder, called *comorbidity*. More than half of the teens with depression, according to Cait Irwin's *Monochrome Days*, often have two or more disorders at once. Depression may also be accompanied by anxiety disorder, or a learning disorder, a substance-abuse disorder, sex addiction, eating disorder, attention-deficit disorder, or a conduct disorder.

Causes

Depression does not have a single cause, according to Dr. James Whitney Hicks in *50 Signs of Mental Illness*. An episode of depression, he says, is brought about by stress *in people who have a biological predisposition to the illness*. The chance of developing depression is 2 to 3 times higher if you have a relative who has been diagnosed with major depression. So if, besides a genetic predisposition to depression, you add the stress of family death or someone you love, an abusive childhood or environment, divorce, an absence of someone to talk to, physical disease, or other disorders, the likelihood of episodes of depression is increased.

Treatments

Because depression is rooted in a chemical imbalance within the brain, it makes sense that it responds to the chemical treatment of medications such as Prozac, Paxil, Zoloft and other such drugs which affect nerve cells. Serotonin is one of the pleasure chemical messengers in the brain, and it is thought that low levels of serotonin decrease interest, energy, and pleasure in life.

Because depression is also influenced by life events and patterns of behavior and thought and feeling, psychotherapy (talk therapy or behavioral therapies) is the second main treatment option.

The combination of medication and psychotherapy seems to yield the best results.

Age of Onset

Depression generally presents itself during the teens, but young children may exhibit the same symptoms. Neglected babies have been diagnosed with depression. Older people may not have had symptoms earlier, due perhaps to well-lived lives, but the onset of depression can occur at every age. The average age of onset for major depressive disorder is mid-twenties, according to the *DSM*.

Course and Prognosis

According to the *DSM*, the course of Major Depressive Disorder is variable. Some people have isolated episodes separated by years, some have clusters of episodes, others have increasingly frequent episodes.

Diagnosis

A Major Depressive Episode must be distinguished from a mood disorder caused by a medical condition or a psychological trauma like death, divorce, or isolation. Proper diagnosis is always key to treatment.

BIPOLAR DISORDER (MANIC DEPRESSION)

Definition

Bipolar disorder is characterized by Major Depressive Episodes (see above characteristics) alternating with periods lasting at least a week of abnormally and persistently elevated, hyper-energetic, possibly irritable moods referred to as Manic Episodes. Bipolar Disorder, with its alternating episodes of major depression and mania, is a recurrent disorder, with lifetime episodes. The manic episodes of the disturbance that alternate with depressions include the following characteristics.

Manic Episode Symptoms

- Inflated self-esteem or grandiosity.

- Decreased need for sleep.

- Pressured, rushed, loud speech, flighty ideas.

- Happy, cheerful, high and expansive mood—may even appear slightly drunk.

- Increased activity, excessive enthusiasm and energy directed toward sex, play, interpersonal relationships, work, activities.

- Unstoppable chatter with friends, family, strangers, salespeople, leaping from topic to topic .

- Uncritical self-confidence, grandiose delusions of accomplishable possibilities for future work, position, travel, possessions, relationships with public figures, heroes, even God.

- If thwarted or argued with, irritable, hostile, teary.

- Poor judgment in money, people, situations, such as overspending, infidelity, assaultive or illegal behavior, bad business judgment.

- Excessive sociability, middle-of-the-night phoning or dashing around.

- Manic episodes in adolescents are more likely to include psychotic features and may include school truancy, antisocial behavior, school failure, and substance abuse.

● Mixed episodes are characterized by meeting criteria for both Manic Episodes and Major Depressive Episodes nearly every day.

● Many people with bipolar disorder find that seasons affect their episodes and depend on the amount of daylight. Depression in the fall and winter may respond to light therapy.

Causes

As with most mental illnesses, we don't know precisely what causes bipolar disorder. Genetics play a large part; you are ten times more likely to develop the illness if a close family member has the diagnosis. As with depression bipolar disorder may be a brain chemical imbalance that can be corrected with medication and cognitive behavioral therapy, talk therapy, geared toward correcting destructive behaviors and thereby reorganizing the nerve pathways of the brain.

Treatments

A combination of medications has worked best for some. The use of antidepressants for the depression, and lithium for the manic episodes has worked in many cases. Psychotherapy can be essential for bipolar disorder, as one of its main characteristics is the inability to think things through very clearly, especially if there is stress. Clearer insight than one's own is very helpful.

Age of Onset

Depressions usually precede manic episodes in the lives of those with bipolar disorder, and those can begin in childhood. The manic episodes usually begin in adolescence. The presenting symptoms, for instance grandiose and persecution delusions, irritability, agitation, and all kinds of acting out from shopping sprees to substance abuse, can be confused with adolescence itself, so that often bipolar disorder is not correctly diagnosed until the mid-twenties.

Course and Prognosis

According to the *DSM*, the course of Bipolar Disorder, like Major Depressive Disorder, is variable. Some people may have lifelong revolving episodes, some may have episodes every few years.

Diagnosis

Bipolar Disorder, like Major Depressive Disorder, must be distinguished from those disorders with similar symptoms that are due to physical, medical conditions. Multiple sclerosis, thyroid conditions, stroke or other physical trauma can cause depression and mood swings as well. As can substance abuse and other addictions.

Chapter Four

THE DISORDERED BRAIN

Anxiety, Obsessive-Compulsive Disorder, Personality, And Behavioral Disorders

Don't Suffer Alone

Most of the disorders in this chapter usually develop in adolescence or early adulthood. The sooner you recognize symptoms and report them to a trusted parent, teacher, counselor, or friend, the sooner you can be properly diagnosed and treated. Don't sit around with an unbalanced mind any longer than you would a broken leg.

Whether treatment includes medication, talk, behavioral, or other therapies, it is up to you to take responsibility for and participate in your own recovery. You can't walk unsupported with a broken leg: you can't live unsupported with a broken personality. With any luck you have a strong support system. But even without luck, *you have yourself to depend on to find the help and support you need.*

ANXIETY DISORDERS

Without anxiety, you would be dead. Anxiety is based in being alert and careful enough to stay alive. There is a progression from careful to crippled that mental health experts monitor for anxiety disorder, but everyone experiences anxiety. Those feelings of stress, nervousness, panic, butterflies, the jitters, freaking out are based simply on belonging to the human race. We humans are a conscious animal. This means we not only worry about the present, we consciously remember our past anxieties, and we imagine future possible problems.

Definition

Anxiety disorder is one of the most common mental health problems. There are 19 million of us. Anxiety is common to most other mental illnesses, as well as being a chronic illness of its own. Anxiety is more than just an ordinary and appropriate nervousness such as you might feel before a test, speaking to an audience, meeting new people, or facing something physically new or unknown.

Symptoms

Anxiety disorder floods the system with more than normal alarm. Everyone knows the feeling of anxiety. Something known or unknown has gone wrong or soon will go wrong. The body reacts with physical symptoms: headaches, tense muscles, sweating, stomach and intestinal problems from nausea to diarrhea. Your blood pressure and pulse may rise, your heart may pound. You may shake uncontrollably. You may have difficulty focusing on work, on people's words. Tears may come easily, sleep not at all. You feel overwhelmed by life, by expectations, your own and other people's. You go from self-pity to anger to fear. Chronic, constant anxiety can be mild or absolutely disabling.

Further Symptoms

Anxiety may accompany other mental disorders. The feelings of worthlessness, the hopelessness and guilt of depression, the phobias of anxiety disorder, the hallucinations of schizo-phrenia, the physical problems of accident or illness may also cause anxiety. But these conditions have different treatments. So in diagnosis, it is important to distinguish between an ac-companying anxiety and what is called generalized anxiety disorder.

Medication, psychotherapy, exercise, meditation, yoga, the right food, and a deep investigation into your own and ev-eryone else's all too human anxiousness will help. Just being a human being, feeling insecure and lost among the stars, is enough to make anyone who thinks about these things deep-ly anxious sometimes. The question is whether anxiety is crip-pling you or just helping you stay safe.

If anxiety is limiting what you do, if it makes your world smaller, if the physical sensations caused by anxiety interfere with your life, your friendships, your capacity to be part of life, you may have a problem you need to address.

Treatment Depends on Type of
Anxiety Disorder Based on Symptoms

Anxiety disorders come in different varieties and degrees. As noted in the *DSM*, types of severe anxieties must be sorted out so that they can be treated properly, from medications to exposure therapy to talk therapy, from exercise to just breathing into a brown paper bag when panic attacks. Some of the anxiety disorders are:

1. **Panic Disorder.** Panic attacks are intense, sudden episodes of fear without necessary cause, accompanied by shortness of breath, rapid heartbeat, pulse, chest pain, dizziness, nausea, diarrhea, sweating, trembling, hot and cold flashes. This is a very intense form of anxiety disorder, with body and mind fully engaged in threat response.

2. **Phobias.** Phobias are anxiety disorders in relation to specific conditions. Agoraphobia is the fear of open spaces, an intense anxiety about being somewhere uncomfortable from which there is no escape. There are people who are simply afraid to leave their homes. Other people may be phobic about a particular animal, heights, water, the dark, fears about social situations in which they feel inadequate, judged, blamed for their performance, personal appearance, any judgmental criticism, often worrying long after the exposure or event.

3. **Post-Traumatic Stress Disorder (PTSD).** Exposure to serious trauma, emotional or physical harm, one's own or as a witness to other people's harm. Fear and anxiety, nightmares, flashbacks, memories, frightening thoughts, even physical or mental paralysis may result. Loud or sudden noises, movements, a sudden touch can shatter the nerves and trigger painful memories of war, accidents, fire, rape or other physical or psychological abuse.

4. **Anxiety Disorder Accompanying Obsessive-Compulsive Disorder.** OCD will be further described. It is characterized by obsessional thoughts that won't go away and compulsive behaviors meant to relieve the obsessional thoughts. Since the repetitive behaviors meant to relieve the repetitive thoughts don't work, the behaviors (such as hand washing, wall-touching, counting, list-making) have to be repeated over and over again.

5. **Substance-Induced Anxiety in Withdrawal.** It is said by many experts that alcoholism and drug-abuse involve OCD—relief from fear and anxiety is never achieved so the abuse is repeated.

Major Causes of Anxiety

● **Genetics:** our ancestors survived because our brains are wired to supply a rush of adrenaline when threatened, so we will fight or flee perceived threats.

● **Brain chemistry:** the type, amount, and movement of your brain's chemicals.

● **Your personal outer environment as well as genetic human history:** ordinary stresses from home and school life; deeper stresses of violence, abuse, addiction, mental or physical illness.

Your Self as Cause

Your self is a great cause of anxiety. Your own inner environment, your thoughts, your feelings, your memories, your reactions to what happens to you may scare the life out of you. While all humans and human brains are pretty much alike, a little too much of this or that experience outwardly, a little too much reactive hypersensitivity inwardly, too much or too little of a particular brain chemical, a brain wiring flaw, a physical disease—and you may experience more than average anxiety.

Keep talking to one another and share your lives with one another. Use each other as mirrors to look at yourselves. Dialogue is a good basis to begin understanding your self, and to discover if you need professional help.

STORY
HIPPOPOTAMUS: A LIFETIME OF ANXIETY

❝I couldn't spell hippopotamus. I was in the second grade. The now familiar symptoms crept through my body like fire ants under my skin. I trembled and shivered, my stomach filled with a large, heavy, hot stone, my blood raced, my head ached, my heart pounded, I felt as if I was gasping for breath, and the more I tried, the less I could concentrate.

My mother was called. I was not only taken out of that school, I was sent to a school where I didn't have to spell hippopotamus and where they understood general anxiety disorder and panic attacks

I think I was about five years old when my intense fears became apparent to me. My family—my mother, father, and older brother—had just moved to a new and much larger New York City apartment from our small, sunny apartment where I had shared a room with my brother. My new home was in a darker, older building, and I didn't like the way it smelled. I was assigned to my own room, to me a separate cell, for the first time. It did not face outward over the quiet, tree-lined avenue as the other bedrooms did, but looked out into shadows. Out of my window, I could see the courtyard, big enough to be inviting for a young child to play in, so small, however, that I could see across into neighbors' windows. Frightened, I understood that this meant they could see into mine! Among my fears was that an evil neighbor would extend a plank long enough to reach my window, use to it invade my room at night, and hurt me. I lived in terror of being in or causing pain. I lived in terror of being without my mother's protection. When she went out at night or traveled, I supplied us both with scraps of notepaper and pencil stubs to keep the connection to her.

Anxiety is intensely distracting. In my teens, rather than being able to focus in class or on my homework, I worried constantly over what I myself or others meant when they spoke. I worried whether I myself or someone else had been intentionally or unintentionally cruel. I agonized over not fitting in, and not knowing how to be comfortable in my own skin, while it seemed to me everyone else in their teens was just skating through their lives with ease.

My college memories are misted with a film of obsessive anxiety and isolation. I could just get through class, before I was totally enveloped in panic and needed the protective privacy of my dorm room. I developed an eating disorder to add to my psychological pain and anxiety. I binged and purged what I ate. I self-medicated my tormenting loneliness and tried to relieve my anxieties with drugs, alcohol, excessive spending, and lovers. The relief granted for short intervals would have been worth the price I had to pay, only I became addicted to my escapes. I had to have more and more of everything to medicate my anxiety, until my life became completely unmanageable. There were longer and longer periods of anxiety-ridden, lonely depressions.

I managed, nevertheless, to earn two graduate degrees and licensing in my field. My work and my newly acquired addiction to exercise and compulsive busyness gave me enough of an endorphin high to partially relieve my obsessive anxiety and compulsive behaviors and addictions. Eventually, I found my way into CBT—cognitive behavioral therapy—to learn to change my ways of thinking as well as my behaviors, and participate in two twelve-step programs. One was for my substance dependency, the other for my dependency on other people and the need for their approval. I continue to exercise. I've gone back and forth between martial arts, yoga, the gym, running—whatever appeals to me at the time. I've been advised to sleep and eat regularly, and not to get too tired or lonely. During very stressful periods, there are medications prescribed by my psychiatrist I can take.

I still have GAD—generalized anxiety disorder. I'm told my brain chemistry, my neural pathways of anxiety will always be prey to more of the normal fight-or-fight adrenaline all creatures need to increase energy on order to avoid danger and survive. But now I know what to do about it when my system is flooded with panic chemicals, how to think about it, and most important, that my chemistry need never again freeze me in my tracks, fill me with rage, or take over my life.

My coping skills are pretty good. I have even learned to use some of that extra adrenaline for better performance, even for a natural high. But I know now when to tell myself enough is enough and settle down.**"**

OBSESSIVE-COMPULSIVE DISORDER

Obsessive-compulsive disorder is listed in many mental illness books as both an anxiety disorder and a personality disorder. It is also a component of addiction disorders from alcoholism to drug dependence, gambling, sexual and gender disorders, addictions to games, danger, romance, electronic worlds, overeating—any pain and suffering escape and relief activity that takes over more of a person's life than is mentally and physically healthy and balanced.

My own obsessive-compulsive disorder is part of my alcoholism, my bipolar mental illness, my compulsive anxiety to complete whatever I start. It is also a component of my life as a writer. It feels to me as if I have to write in order to breathe, to stay alive. I get obsessively anxious if I don't write, and am compelled to write again.

Studies have indicated that OCD is a component of the lives of artists of all kinds, musicians, painters, athletes, and performers. It may well underlie the mental states of all extremely talented and successful people with a compelling drive to succeed at what they do, and repeat that behavior over and over again.

Obsessions are persistent ideas, thoughts, impulses, or images that cause intense anxiety and distress. They intrude unwanted, uncontrollably into the mind. These can be aggressive (wanting to smack or torture someone), obscene (wanting to pee on the couch), sexual (repeated mental pornography), fearful (terrors of rape, murder, torture, fire).

Compulsions are repetitive behaviors used to prevent or reduce the anxiety caused by the obsessions. These can take many forms: prayer; checking and rechecking; counting or lining things up; safety rituals of all kinds from chronic washing of hands to never deviating from routes or schedules or habits.

Dangers in OCD

Some obsessive-compulsive disorders threaten the lives of others, such as pyromania (setting fires), kleptomania (compulsive stealing), pedophilia (sexual molestation of young children), sadism (compulsive need to inflict pain). Some impulse-control disorders are psychologically and physically distressing primarily to the sufferer, such as cutting oneself or compulsive pulling out of one's body hair (trichotillomania).

A primary cause of personal suffering from obsessive-compulsive disorder are the rituals conceived by the sufferer as necessary to ward off danger. These rituals, imagined to be protective, can consume hours of the day, years in the lives of people with OCD. In minor form, such rituals can include having to straighten magazines on a table, making sure all the labels of nail polish and perfume bottles face forward on a shelf, multiple checking of locks on windows and doors, and hundreds of other varieties of safety rituals. OCD is responsible for avoidant (phobic) behavior as well as performance behavior. Being too afraid of open spaces to leave the house (agoraphobia), fear of water, and sleep terror disorders are among them.

A major characteristic of people with OCD is a constant need for reassurance to support their constant need for repetition. Any resistance to the repetition of their rituals from hand-washing to drug use is met with high anxiety, anger, or both.

Performing compulsions to avoid anxiety may consume the life of people with OCD and lead to serious interference with relationships, school, work, and all the ordinary activities of life. A compulsive extra hand-washing or two to avoid the obsessive anxiety of contamination is one thing. An extra bottle of vodka or being unable to leave the house to avoid anxiety is another.

The good news is that OCD is treatable. Anti-anxiety medication and several kinds of behavioral and talk therapy, support groups, meditation, and physical exercise can relieve both obsessions and compulsions so they do not interfere with or destroy a happy and useful life. Latest statistics, according to Dr, Hicks, show that one in forty people suffer from the intrusive obsessive thoughts and compulsive behaviors of this illness, making OCD the most common mental disorder after depression.

You are not alone when you have intrusive, anxious, unwanted thoughts, or you worry about the smell of your armpits when you hook up, or that you'll shout out an obscene word in class, or whether you remembered to put on your clothes in the exact right order for safety's sake.

Compare notes with your friends. You'll discover they have these thoughts, too. If you don't get drunk, stoned, immobilized, or crazy over them, chances are you'll be all right. If your thoughts drive you mad, get help.

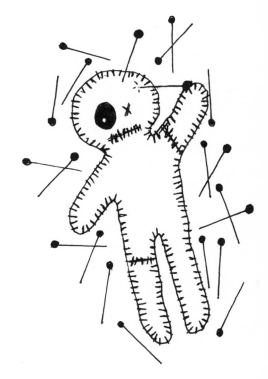

STORY
A SON'S OCD

❝I was not the son my father wanted. We both wanted heroics from me. He wanted a rich and successful businessman. I just wanted to save the world.

Our joint disappointment in me, in combination with whatever genes ran in the family, produced a virulent case of my lifetime of Obsessive-Compulsive Disorder. I felt unsafe without my father's approval. So my OCD was all about safety. What I was trying to do was counter what I thought was the basic flaw in my nature.

I always thought that inside me was a fatal flaw, something in my nature that was inherently wrong. This was because I was certainly not the son my parents wanted in so many ways, and because I was always afraid something horrible was going to spill out of me and contaminate everything and everyone I touched. Not only was I unsafe to myself, but everyone around me. I had no idea how to fix what was wrong with me. I only knew I wasn't safe, I wasn't okay, I wasn't lovable the way I was.

It was therefore important that I look good, not physically necessarily, but in terms of being adequate and competent.

I wanted no one to know I was fatally flawed.

I had been born prematurely. Nobody touched me the first two months of my life. I lived in a plastic box. Studies have shown that lack of physical nurturing in babies affects the neural wiring in the emotional parts of the brain. I personally turned out to be a weird little kid.

At the age of 12, I began making lists. I made list after list of everything I had to do, from brushing my teeth to getting dressed and so on throughout the day, at home and at school. I also broke up the lists and made lists of lists. I made lists of my clothes, of safe paths and zones in my life to walk to school, to friends' houses, on errands, wherever I went when I left my home.

As well as lists for safety's sake, I had routines for safety. I had to walk the same paths, wear certain clothes for luck, so I had lucky socks, pants, and shirts. All these rituals were to keep me safe from the unknown harm waiting to punish me for being flawed.

At the time, and all the time, I just thought I was a bad kid. I didn't do things right. And I was the oldest son, so a lot was expected.

"Oh, son," they sighed in disappointment. Over and over and over again.

It felt as if nothing I ever did was good enough. As a teen, I was to get good marks. Later, I was to marry well, I was to become an important, titled businessman. Only I was interested in the wrong things. I liked music, girls, civil rights, and nature.

"What an idiot! What are you doing!"

I was interested in the wrong girls.

I was fierce in sports, but I wasn't a killer, and it was all right with me if other people won.

And because I had asthma, I even breathed wrong.

By the time I got to college, I knew I really didn't want a business life. I wanted to become a civil rights worker, a union organizer, in some way involved with what humanity suffered from. Not one of the inflictors.

I knew what the expectations were, what the games were, how to intuit what parents, teachers, women wanted. I played at them, looking for a way to be safe. But for all the games, the safety zones, the lucky clothes, and the lists, I was never the son my parents wanted and I always felt fundamentally unsafe and unloved.

I was desperate in my need to be loved and to be filled up by love.

My first addiction was to girls.

And after the girls, booze.

There was no way middle-class expectations were going to fill my cup, so I escaped altogether. The sixties with its freedom cries helped.

I did, in fact, get my Ph.D. in Counseling. I do, in fact, what I can about human suffering. I finally found a good mate. I joined a twelve-step program, eventually went on a vision quest supervised by a shaman to face down my demons. Cognitive behavioral therapy, a lot of talking through instead of acting out my feelings, both as student and teacher, giver and receiver of counseling, has gentled my terrors of feeling unsafe and made my compulsive behaviors, my OCD containable.

Now, I think I am as happy as humans get to be—which to me means being of whatever help I can to others and to help them get through their pain as I got through mine, with the help of counseling, meditation, and the ongoing therapy of sharing with others.**"**

PERSONALITY DISORDERS

In her book *The Courage to Lead: Mental Illnesses and Addictions*, Hannah Carlson says, " These disorders are characterized by a lifetime of conflict and distress. The pain is caused by the faulty perception of oneself and one's relationship with others...and leads to disappointment and unfulfilled expectations."

The major problem of people with personality disorders is their difficulty in seeing either themselves or other people accurately. This flawed perception makes it very difficult for them to change. Personality disorders usually develop in adolescence or early adulthood, and if untreated lead to loneliness and anger, lifelong misunderstandings in relationships, even mental hospitals and prisons. Often, people diagnosed with a personality disorder have more than one. Someone with a borderline personality disorder, for instance, may also have an antisocial or narcissistic personality disorder.

The major position of people with personality disorders is that *everything is always someone else's fault*. What they fail to see are their own misperceptions.

Antisocial Personality Disorder

People with this disorder feel as if society's rules don't apply to them, at home, at school, at work, in general. Some lie, cheat, and steal. Some rape, fight, and bully others. Some live only to satisfy to their own rules, ideas, and pleasures without any regard for their victims.

Half to three-quarters of prison inmates, according to psychiatric studies, have an antisocial personality disorder that makes them particularly dangerous. This extreme is called psychopathic personality. Remorseless, manipulative, violent, abusive, fraudulent behaviors characterize this mental disorder. Its natural environment is organized crime, terrorism, street gangs, illegal business dealings, the spy business.

Sadism goes even beyond conscienceless behavior. It describes the actual pleasure taken in rape, torture, arson, bullying, coercion. There may even be a component of sexual excitement involved.

Scientists have found family genetic factors as well as environmental factors such as a childhood spent in a war zone, poverty, in foster homes or prison for the antisocial traits of oppositional behavior. These traits include anger, impulsiveness, a lack of respect or empathy for the rights and feelings of others. Lack of responsibility or remorse, reckless disregard for others, repeated physical fights or assaults, repeated lying, all are indicators.

Conduct problems as the basis for antisocial personality disorders may be found as young as early childhood, though the full-blown disorder usually appears during the teen years. But antisocial behaviors may emerge in an adult as a result of accident, damage to the frontal lobes, the seat of judgment.

Once established, unfortunately, antisocial personality disorder has not been proved treatable. If you feel endangered by someone's abusive behavior, call the police.

Bullying, a form of disregard for and violation of others' rights, may be physical or verbal. This disorder may begin in childhood and carry on through adolescence and adulthood. Bullies of any kind, in school, on the street, bosses at work, even parents or siblings at home may take a sadistic pleasure in making others suffer. Don't take bullying passively. No one has a right to hurt you physically or verbally. Report it to someone you trust. Get help.

Borderline Personality Disorder

The most important indication of this disorder is the instability of personal relationships. And the frantic need not to be abandoned. Even the perception of the possibility of abandonment, such as lateness or criticism activates fears. People with borderline personality disorder fall in love or imagine a caregiver or best friend instantly. They quickly become too needy or feel rejected, and move on to the next idealized person. It is one of the most widespread disorders for women, especially for women in addiction recovery programs and in prisons. Instant intimacy is an attachment disorder.

Frantic efforts to avoid abandonment may include suicidal behaviors, attention-getting behaviors such as cutting, histrionic emotional outbursts when a date or a meeting comes to its natural end—anything to avoid being alone. This disorder is often accompanied by excessive gambling, binge-eating, substance abuse, sex addiction—any behavior that helps them avoid the panic and despair of being left alone, of the chronic feelings of emptiness.

Bipolar Disorders Are Mood
Disorders that Affect the Personality

Disturbances in moods that swing from deep depression to high, manicky episodes characterize this group of disorders: Bipolar I, Bipolar II, and the slightly less extreme mood swings of Cyclothalmic Disorder. The differences lie mostly in duration and degree.

Bipolar disorders are recurrent disorders—more than 90% of people who have a single manic episode go on to have more of them. About 70% of manic episodes occur just before or just after a major depressive episode. The cycling of depressive and manic episodes may be rapid or slow, with four or more episodes in a given year.

Suicide occurs in 10%-15% of people with Bipolar I Disorder, according to the *DSM*. Child abuse, spouse abuse, or other violent behavior may occur during manic episodes. School truancy, school failure, work failures, antisocial behavior, the breaking up of relationships, sleep problems, anorexia/bulimia, ADHD behaviors, panic disorders, social phobias, and substance-abuse related disorders are among the problems associated with bipolar disorders.

About 10%-15% of adolescents with recurrent depression will go on to develop bipolar disorders. Unlike Major Depression, more common in females, bipolar disorders occurs equally in males and females.

Although the majority of people who suffer from bipolar disorders return to a fully functioning level between episodes, some 20%-30% continue to have mood swings and interpersonal difficulties.

It is important to distinguish between bipolar disorders based on medical conditions (such as multiple sclerosis or stroke) and substance-induced mood disorders, and Bipolar Disorder based on true Major-Depressive, Manic, or Mixed Episode Bipolar Disorder. The treatment, both in medication and therapy will differ.

It is equally important to differentiate psychotic disorders like schizophrenia from bipolar disorders. Especially in the teen years, symptoms like grandiosity, persecution delusions, irritability, and agitation may present themselves in several mental diseases.

Hannah Carlson reports that borderline and bipolar mental illnesses use about 80% of this country's money and resources in psychiatric wards, doctors' services, and emergency rooms.

Dependent Personality Disorder is characterized by an excessive clinging, a need to be taken care of, a self-perception of being unable to function without the help of others. **Histrionic Personality Disorder** is also characterized by attention-seeking, manipulative behaviors and deep feelings of emptiness and abandonment. **Narcissistic Personality Disorder**, with its grandiosity, and need for admiration, lack of empathy for others, is also difficult to change. And **Avoidant Personality Disorder**, with its fears of disapproval, criticism, rejection that cause the sufferer to avoid work, school, relationships, needs much work to change, as it can stem from early childhood fear of new people and situations and worsen with adolescence. **Paranoid Personality Disorder** infects those who have it with the belief that others are exploiting, harming, or out to get them, untrusting, unforgiving, resentful. All these disorders interfere with stable, long-lasting relationships.

As with all people with personality disorders, insight into their own behavior is limited, and to make and sustain lasting relationships is difficult. Change is slow, but possible with therapy and hard work.

Obviously, many of the personality disorders are co-occurring, and also co-occur with addictive behaviors. Addictive behaviors are used as escapes from the suffering personality disorders cause.

Other Disorders

All of the mental illnesses and disorders we've discussed so far create disordered behaviors.

Actually, just being in possession of a human brain creates disordered behaviors. This comes, as we've discovered, from our inability so far to understand ourselves and our still-primitive instincts, and to regulate our behavior so we don't suffer and make other people suffer. This comes also, as we've said, through faulty or damaged nerve wiring and chemical behavior in the brain.

The Human Brain Is Plastic, Moldable, Changeable

Our brains are not made of cement. Their wiring and chemistry can and do change. Every little thing, every insight and new behavior affects our brains, our brains' neurological (nerve) wiring, and our brain chemistry. Among the reasons psychotropic medication (psych meds), therapy, changes in living patterns, education, diet, proper breathing, and exercise work in recovery is because the brain's wiring can change in healthy ways as well as be damaged by defects in heredity or environment.

Insight into Our Thought Patterns,
Feelings, and Behavior Can Cause Mutation
in Our Brains through Actual Rewiring

Attention Heals and Rewires Your Brain

The healing way of living is, as we have said, to pay a great deal of attention to our thoughts, our feelings, and our behaviors. Attention and insight into violent or unhealthy behaviors, thoughts, and feelings will end them the moment they occur, and every time they arise again. A lot of defective or inappropriate behaviors won't vanish forever, but they can be stopped every time they come up. A good example is the life of a recovering alcoholic, drug, food or sex addict. Some of us will never not have the disease of alcoholism, but when the thought of a drink comes up, we just don't act on it.

Our work on ourselves, whether we are mentally ill, healthy, or average is to pay this kind of attention to what we say, do, feel, and think, so we don't act out in ways that harm ourselves or others. (See *Understand Your Self* by Dale Carlson.)

Many brain scientists point out that insight changes the brain's wiring, actually mutates the brain, so we can stop causing ourselves and other people unnecessary psychological suffering.

Some Further Behavior Disorders

Body Dysmorphic Disorder: Perception of oneself as thinner, fatter, uglier, prettier—different from what one is.

Gender Identity Disorder: Perception of being male in a female body or female in a male body. (There is debate about whether this should be considered a disorder.)

Sexual Disorders: Exhibitionism, fetishism, sexual masochism, sexual sadism, transvestic fetishism (cross dressing), voyeurism, pedophilia, necrophilia (being only able to function sexually with the dead and unresponsive).

Neglect/Abuse Disorders: Problems arising from abuse or neglect: attachment disorders, bonding problems, antisocial behaviors.

Sleep Disorders, Grief Disorders, Dissociative and Other Identity Disorders, Medication-Induced Disorders, Psychosocial and Relational Disorders, and more.

Chapter Five

ADDICTION DISORDERS, SUBSTANCES & BEHAVIORS

Alcohol, Drugs, Food, Sex/Romance, Gambling, Danger, Shopping, Sports, TV, Video Games, Internet, One's Self

Three Causes of Addiction: Genes, Environment, and You

No one pours a drink or a pill down your throat. No one inhales for you. No one injects you illegally. And no one stands in the way of recovery and treatment but you.

You may have inherited the genes for addiction, you may have grown up in an environment like a war zone. It is still all up to you. Repeated use, as well as genes and environment, are the causes of addiction.

So is attitude. *I always thought if I wanted something desperately, I had to have it, whether the craving was for a drink, a drug, a boyfriend or a success. I thought that the craving would never stop, would make me crazy, until it was satisfied. It took treatment in recovery for me to learn these three things:*

- that the craving was actually bearable without giving in

- that the craving was based on my having given in to the previous craving (one drink or cigarette caused the chemical craving for the next so the only way to stop the pain of craving was to stop using)

- most amazing, the craving would pass whether I gave in to it or not

"Lesson? I didn't, and don't, have to let my brain kill me!" as it says in *Addiction: The Brain Disease* by Dale Carlson and Hannah Carlson.

WHAT IS ADDICTION?

Definition
Addiction is an obsession over something you feel compelled to act on. Mental *obsession* and physical *compulsion* are the key words. OCD underlies addiction. It has been said, for instance, that alcoholism is a mental obsession over alcohol together with a compulsion to drink it.

Symptoms

Research has shown that all drugs of abuse and abuse behavior activate the brain's pleasure pathways. Food, exercise, lovemaking, music, and whatever else turns you on, activate a surge in the level of the brain's transmitter dopamine. The experience is then "logged into the brain's limbic system, which, in addition to being the center for pleasure and emotion, houses key memory and motivation circuits. This is what the brain's dopamine pathway does; it records both the actual experience of pleasure and ensures that the behaviors that led to it are remembered and repeated, " say the editors John Hoffman and Susan Froemke of *Addiction: Why Can't they Just Stop?* based on an HBO documentary on drug abuse. (See Drug and Alcohol Chart, pages 192-195.)

Remember that the whole dopamine system evolved from the evolutionary biological imperative of survival. Food meant survival, sex meant survival, and going back for more of both meant survival of whatever species you belonged to.

The first time we take alcohol or drugs—including caffeine and nicotine as well as party or club drugs, over-the-counter or prescription drugs—dopamine levels spike higher than they do with food or even sex, and that experience is remembered. It is stored in the brain's hippocampus (memory) and amygdala (emotion). The spiked pleasure levels will recede, but they are recorded in the brain's nerve memory.

The next time we use, the spike is lower, the crash is deeper. After repeated drug use, the brain no longer produces its own adequate supply of dopamine. It craves more and more of the addicted substance, fooled into thinking the drug (or even the behavioral addiction to food, sex, gambling) is necessary for comfort, even functional survival.

The Three Symptoms of Addiction

1.   Increased dependency—more intense craving: an addict wants, even needs, more and more of the substance or behavior to maintain emotional and physical balance.

2.   Increased tolerance—more and more of the drug is needed to get high, sometimes in amounts that would be lethal to a nonuser, leading to even more of the addictive behavior.

3.   Withdrawal symptoms—without the drug, depression follows, along with uncomfortable, even painful physical and emotional symptoms. The use of drugs reduces your body's production of its own endorphins, its own pleasure chemicals, so you cannot make yourself feel good, or even comfortable or pain-free. Brain damage, damage to the brain's nerve circuits from drugs, may be permanent.

Stigma

Just as there must be no stigma attached to any other mental disorder, there must be no stigma or prejudice attached to the disease of addiction. Some people can drink or use for a time and move beyond it—some people's chemistry gets caught in addiction. We have a nasty habit as humans of rejecting anyone who isn't like ourselves in color, behavior, speech, origins, whatever. Rejecting others seems to make us feel superior, or at least safe from any form of contamination. Especially in our teens, we follow the leader. We are a pack animal. We herd. Sheep who are a different color, who behave in a different manner, are often rejected or stigmatized. The trouble with sheep is, when one leader goes off the cliff, all follow. *Don't follow the leader.*

Genius Is Also Abnormal

Genius IQ and talent are also due to abnormal circuitry, just as are mental disorders and addiction. Albert Einstein was slow to develop speech and is thought to have had Asperger's social disabilities, but he understood $E=mc^2$. Beethoven suffered depression, Mozart is thought to have been not only an alcoholic but bipolar. The great artist Van Gogh has been diagnosed with schizophrenia, seizures, and alcoholism. Abraham Lincoln suffered depression. Michael Jackson's genius was accompanied by BDD, body dysmorphic disorder and addiction. The list is endless. Just to be a genius, a talented artist, a great leader, philosopher, gifted performer or athlete makes you just as much a freak of nature as any other difference from the ordinary. So be careful who you pick on or stigmatize. Disorders can make you special. Talent and genius, often accompanied by other mental disorders, are just as abnormal.

Life is full enough of random cruelties. Don't add to them with your own. When you start to feel superior to addicts and alcoholics, remember that substance addiction is not only a disease of thought and emotional states. It is a physical disease like any other, diabetes or heart conditions or allergies, you can inherit or acquire. And, like other diseases, it is, if not curable, certainly treatable.

Needs and Greeds

For survival, we are all programmed to avoid pain as well as seek pleasure. If you're cold, find a coat or a hug. If you're hungry, eat. These are physical pains, and we cope.

Psychological pain and conflicting drives, needs, and greeds are more difficult to handle. We want security, yet yearn for freedom. Each of us feels lonely, yet wants to be special and unique. We're so attached to our people, places, and things, that we live in desperate fear of losing them. All humans suffer from conflict and pain. And nature says, *stop the pain, get out of the conflict.*

All human beings organize a working personality so it can more or less function in the world: it either deals with or escapes its pains and conflicts. This is perfectly natural.

It is only when this natural behavior gets out of control and turns into an addiction that we need to be concerned.

Causes

1.   **Genes.** Ways of dealing with pain tend to run in families, so check out your family for the ways your relatives handled their distress. Did they deal with it, or escape into drugs, alcohol, gambling, sex, food, constant busyness, shopping, television. There are long lists of escapes used by human beings to numb pain.

2.   **Environment.** Childhood cruelty, an environment of drug and alcohol use can trigger addiction

3.   **Previous behavior.** Not even your own past behavior has to ruin your future. You can take control of your life.

No matter how it feels, biology is not destiny and environment and past behavior are not destiny. Treatment and help are always available to change behavior and rewire your brain circuits. The human brain is plastic, capable of change.

Treatment and Recovery: to an Addict, Heaven and Hell

For an alcoholic/addict, the only cure is to STOP.

This is often painful, usually terrifying, always hard. But hard as it is, to go on using is harder. Only more misery, loneliness, fear, madness, homelessness, sickness, prison, and death await you.

I know. Dale Carlson has been a recovering alcoholic/addict, clean and dry for 35 years.

If you can't stop drinking and using on your own (and most people don't have enough information about the physical, emotional and psychological stress involved), ask for help.

1. Talk to people you can trust to help you stop.

2. Telephone. Use the phone numbers at the back of this book. There are fellow alcoholics and addicts who answer phones and will understand and direct you to treatment and meetings near you to meet other teens who have been through the same thing. They will understand and help you.

ADDICTION TO BEHAVIORS

What Is Addictive Behavior?

"An addictive behavior is something you feel compelled to do over and over again. It is an action based on an emotional need, a mental obsession, and a physical compulsion to perform that behavior—again and again and again."—*Addiction: The Brain Disease*, by Dale Carlson and Hannah Carlson.

Alcoholism and drug addiction are the use of external substances to alter inner chemistry. Addictive behaviors also alter the brain's chemistry, but by the repetition of behaviors instead of drug use.

How Does Addictive Behavior Begin?

Addictive behavior might start out as an ordinary activity in your family, like watching television, or among your friends, such as video games or hooking up or eating fast food. Obsessive habits grow out of ordinary activities. But what might begin as an ordinary activity or an experiment can turn into a compulsion so irresistible it wrecks a life.

Addictive behavior can also start, not from pleasure alone, but from a need to escape the fears, worry, anxiety of just living your life. Obsessive activities can begin from an original spurt of dopamine, and other pleasure chemicals in your brain. *You can become as addicted to your own brain chemicals as external ones.*

Possible Addictive Behaviors

A good example of a growing addiction is falling in love. We fall in love, not so much with the other person, as the way the sight and touch of the other person makes our own chemistry dance. And we want more and more of that high, the pulse racing, the butterflies or the burning inside, the flush, the heart pounding, the consuming focus on each other that shuts the rest of the world and its troubles out.

Romance addiction, sex addiction (these may differ), gambling, sports, eating, shopping, TV, internet, electronic games and devices, risk-taking and danger—any activity can turn into the obsessive-compulsive addiction that makes your blood sing. Even hard work, a talent or an art, from schoolwork to writing to painting, anything that produces the excitement of adrenaline coursing through your system, can become an addiction. I'm often convinced, when people ask me, my being a writer is a compulsive-obsessive disorder. I get high when I work. I get depressed when I don't. The same has been said by any number of artists, writers, doctors, scientists, construction workers, long-distance runners, activity addicts.

Underneath the high is also the feeling of temporary suspension from fear and anxiety. There is the feeling of immunity, of safety during the course of an obsessive compulsive addiction to a favored behavior.

For the moment, nothing can touch you.

Addictive Behavior Problems

Addictive behavior may not be the kind that lands you in a concrete prison, but it creates a jail of its own. *Just as with an addiction to drugs and alcohol, it takes over your life. You need more and more sex, or more and more gambling or video game time, or more and more exercise or chocolate or fast food, more and more of whatever, to maintain your high or sense of security.*

This plays havoc with the rest of your life. An addictive behavior is never satisfied. A single visit to the mall or a porn site, a single internet game, a single junk food binge or sex party, is never enough to satisfy the craving, because the satisfaction of one craving wears off and leads to the next. So addiction takes over the time needed for other things, school, work, friendships and family relationships, activities that are necessary for the totality of a healthy life lived with purpose and meaning.

Addiction, whether of substance or behavior, consumes life like fire. Addictive behaviors can lead to the onset of mental illness, like depression and anxiety disorders. Addictive behaviors can lead to health problems, from STD's to obesity. Addictive behaviors can lead to dropping out of school or running away and homelessness, whole ranges of crime convictions—all to provide time and money to indulge the addictive behavior.

Are You a Behavior Addict?

Test yourself. If you want to know whether you are a behavior addict, addicted to a person, place, thing, activity—don't let yourself near it for a day or two. You'll feel anxious, depressed, incomplete, distracted. You'll have difficulty concentrating on anything but the thought of whatever person, place, thing, or activity you are addicted to. You don't have to do anything about these findings. Just observe what happens to you during these experiments in self-understanding to learn what you actually need, and what you only think you need to feel all right.

Recovery—The Good News

We alone among the species can rise above our genes, our environments, our backgrounds, cultures, and conditioned responses.

We alone among species (that we know of so far) can be conscious of our behaviors, through self-awareness, through self-observation, through talking with each other, teaching ourselves and each other new ways of thinking and behaving. And through changing behavior, we change the neural pathways of the brain and create new pathways and new lives for ourselves.

Most of us need support for changing ourselves and our behavior. Think of therapy or support groups as a kind of learning how to reparent yourself. And most of us need reparenting—either because we didn't listen in the first place, or we had the wrong parents, or we had parents who did not know better because their parents didn't know how to live their lives without psychological suffering.

You can learn to undo your own conditioning. And what you learn, teach!

Addiction to Ourselves: Mostly We Are Addicted to Ourselves

Above all, we are addicted to ourselves. We are addicted to our own self-importance, and this may be the most dangerous addiction of all if it is not understood properly. Self-importance physically is based on the oldest of evolution's laws: survive, don't die, STAY ALIVE!

The dangerous part of self-importance is not the physical, but the psychological addiction to ourselves. Addiction is the needing more and more of something to feel all right, to feel safe, to make fear, depression, and anxiety go away. It may begin with the evolutionary imperative LIFE MUST LIVE—but then it translates itself into I MUST LIVE AND TO LIVE I MUST HAVE IMPORTANCE SO THE GROUP WILL PROTECT ME.

So we grow more and more addicted to our own self-importance. By the time we grow into adults of our species, we are all puffed out with ourselves. We have become addicted to our own colors and nationalities, our own opinions, to other people's opinions of us and our popularity, our images of ourselves, our own personal security, to what belongs to us, to our own ideas of how the world and people should be. We are addicted to our own need for security, acceptance, addicted to our own people, family, cultures, homes, to our own possessions.

We think we need to defend all this to stay alive. It's what we've been taught at home, at school, by our leaders. Killer competition may have been necessary 40,000 years ago in the Stone Age when food was scarce, the getting of it dangerous, and the only place to live was a dark and freezing cave. The trouble is, we are still functioning with that Stone Age brain, when a lot of us now have supermarkets and central heating, and if we could learn to share instead of grab and defend, there would be plenty to go around on this Earth. Sadly, we haven't considered this yet, so the fear of losing what we have, of not getting enough, turns us into greedy addicts.

The problem of addiction is: How much is enough? It's when we want more than enough that addiction sets in.

Fear of not getting enough is the beginning of addiction. Once an evolutionary genetic survival tool among many others, fear rather than intelligence can take over the brain and dictate our thoughts and behavior.

Interesting Questions

How many habits, daily rituals, how much stuff, how many friends, possessions could you let go of and still feel safe?

Which views of the world, your family, culture, religion, other people and their colors, countries, religions, money, class, ethnic backgrounds could you change or let of and still feel secure?

What people in your life define you?

Who is important in your life and why?

....

....

....

....

....

....

....

....

....

All these things can become dependencies.

And dependencies are prisons.

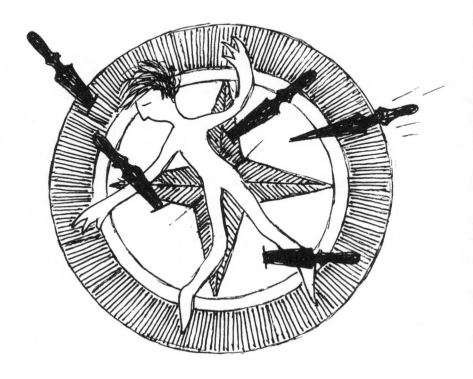

STORY
CAN YOU HELP ME?

"To live at home with her parents was a nightmare Lara could no longer endure.

The daytimes of school and friends, games under falling leaves or snow, homework and texting, calling, or going on-line—the daytimes were fine.

It was the closing in of night that suffocated and sickened her. What might have been to other girls in other families a warm closing in of the evening-lighted nest, was to Lara the first scene in a nightmare drama that played out over and over again in her home.

Her parents had drinks together before dinner, as well as during, and after dinner. This led to arguing, then shouting, then hitting each other or Lara, her younger brother or older sister. Rules for behavior were arbitrary in Lara's home, and often disobeyed and always punished by yelling, slapping, or penalties.

The penalty Lara most often suffered was a late-night visit from her father. The door was opened and closed quietly in the darkness of her bedroom.

"Who's been a bad girl today?" whispered her father's deep voice.

There had to be another life. Lara left home the day after her high school graduation. She took a bus to Las Vegas. In the movies she watched on television, it seemed the one place loud and bright enough to drown out her life. And if the flaring lights and blaring noise were not enough, there were drugs, the flow of alcohol, and sex.

What she wanted was freedom from herself. What she wanted was to overwhelm the noise in her head, the inner arguments, the justifications, the attacks and defenses, the blame, the name-calling, all the voices that inflamed her brain.

She asked a man in the bus station if he knew of a nearby motel. He knew. He took her there. All Lara wanted from him was that he pay her enough to last a few nights' rent in the motel. He volunteered the whiskey, shared what pot he had, and provided Lara with the pattern for her new life.

It was as easy as that to enter hell.

It was even easier to live there. She enjoyed the freedom 'the life' gave her, to pay her own way, to live on her own, to be able to afford her own room, to work, play, and sleep free of disturbance.

All she needed to do was to go out onto the streets of the city, approach a man, raise her eyes to look into his, and say, "Can you help me?"

She stayed clear of the other motel girls. They had 'boyfriends' who controlled them, who took their money. Lara wanted no controls. She had not counted on the most vicious of all controls: the chemistry of her own body—addiction.

After some time, it began to go wrong. It wasn't just that she was arrested twice for possession and prostitution. She made bail. The charges were eventually dismissed. She had sad, dark eyes, a sweet smile. She looked angelic, rather thin and fragile. She could have gotten away with a murder charge.

What went wrong was the slow, devouring process of addiction. Not that Lara knew what was happening to her body, to her mind, heart, and soul. All she knew was that the man who had come back to her motel room the night before to help her, as she had asked—in exchange for sex—was still there at eleven o'clock the next morning. Before he left, he said to Lara, "Let's have one more drink."

Lara never drank in the morning.

That morning she drank.

What was extraordinary to her was, after that morning, she never stopped. The days and nights after that all blurred together somehow, drinking, smoking pot, picking up men in bars, outside brilliantly lit casinos, on dark, back streets. The men were distinguished only by their ability to pay her for rent, her alcohol, her drugs.

It was only by chance that Lara learned about addiction, the biochemical obsession to obey the compulsion to keep a certain level of alcohol and drugs in her blood and flooding her brain. This information came finally with her second arrest for possession and prostitution.

This time, she was sentenced to prison, treatment, and rehabilitation.

It saved her life.

There are easier ways to learn.**JJ**

Chapter Six

SEXUAL & GENDER IDENTITY DISORDERS

Sex Functions

Some of us go through life having sex without thinking too much about the way our sexuality functions. We start in our teens, or just before, wanting to kiss and be held. Then at some point, depending on what everybody else we know is doing or what is permitted in our culture or neighborhood, at some point we go all the way from holding and kissing and touching to full sexual behavior. Nature's instructions on this behavior are pretty automatic, especially in the male. Long before, even during baby years, we have explored our own bodies with our own hands, so we are well acquainted with what gives us pleasure. For most people, it all just happens. Nature has arranged for us to reproduce our own kind, and given us the appropriate responses to our body parts to do so.

Sexual Functions

While everyone has sexual experiences in their own unique fashion, the sexual response cycle is remarkably similar.

1. **Desire**—thinking about sexual acts.

2. **Excitement**—the physiological changes of lubrication and swelling in females, erection in males, to name a few.

3. **Orgasm**—the peak of sexual excitement and pleasure for males and females.

4. **Resolution**—the release of tension and feeling of well-being.

Whenever there is an alteration in the cycle for non-medical, non-physical reasons, it is considered a sexual dysfunction. Too much or too little sexual activity, too much or too little thinking about sex, are considered sexual dysfunction. There can be disorders not only in the desire phase, but in the excitation or orgasmic phases.

A special reminder for teens and young adults: nature has decreed that these are the physical ages best suited for reproduction. It is hardly surprising, therefore, that this reproductive peak is also your sexual peak of desire.

Sexual Dysfunctions

Just as with other body/brain functions, sex can misfire as well.

DSM's Partial List of Sexual Disorders

1.   **Sexual Desire Disorders**: You want sex too much or too little or sex is painful. You can't get or maintain an erection (male), you can't lubricate (female). You have an aversion to sex altogether. You can't have an orgasm, or if you are male, you ejaculate too soon for the female to experience pleasure. You experience pain during sex. Remember that standards of sexual performance and concepts of gender roles during sex vary from culture to culture. Sexual dysfunction may also be due either to a medical condition, the side effect of a drug (party or prescribed), or psychological inhibition. All are treatable.

2.   **Paraphilias**. Sexually arousing fantasies, urges, or behaviors that differ from or harm others. Sexual urges and behaviors involving a) nonhuman objects, b) the suffering or humiliation of oneself or another, c) children or other nonconsenting persons, d) exhibitionism (exposure of genitals), e) voyeurism (observing sexual activity), f) transvestic fetishism (cross-dressing). **Everyone has sexual fantasies. Pornography in art, books, movies, one's own dreams, provocative dress abounds. Sexual expression is human. It is sexual acting-out behavior on others society must monitor.**

3.   **Medical Conditions, Personality Disorder, Relational Problems, and Substance-Induced Conditions.** Any of these can cause disturbances in sexual function.

Gender Identity Disorders

`Nature seems to enjoy variety, however. This is another way of saying, nature usually repeats itself and makes reproductions of its forms. But evolution is based on mutation, the accidental change in genes that may then produce a different color, form, or behavior. Sometimes, the new form functions just fine and produces more like itself. Sometimes the new form is so different, the group doesn't like it or it behaves so differently the group will reject or even kill it. This is how all species evolve and change.

Because it gives the most pleasure (Mother Nature has arranged this to perpetuate life), sex and sexual behavior gets a lot of attention. Any differences in sexual looks, like the size and shape of penises and breasts, attracts notice. Any differences in preferences and performance also attract notice.

If the difference is too marked, people get upset and call the sexual behavior or appearance dysfunctional.

Some people know for a fact that they were born in bodies of the wrong gender. Someone who feels persistent misery socially, psychologically, occupationally about having to live in the body of the wrong gender is suffering identity anguish that requires attention. We think nothing of changing jobs, addresses, clothes, or names according to need or taste. Why do we make such a fuss or create stigma over people born male who identify with female bodies and activities, or people born female who feel entirely male and choose to go through sex changes?

Crossing-dressing, hormonal treatment, plastic surgery are all available for those who want to make a sex change. We think nothing of aging actors who want to look young again having surgery, we think nothing of people who want their noses fixed or their chin lines adjusted, we admire people burned in fires who go through years of reconstruction to feel normal again. Why do we make such a big deal out of a sex change? Gender identity disorder is completely treatable. With counseling to get used to the changes, families and friends can be very supportive.

Sexual Preference Differences

Differences are not disorders. There are boys who like boys instead of girls, and girls who like girls instead of boys. We have all kinds of hair, colors, height, weight, and capacities in the human species. Differences in sexual preferences are just another pleasant variation, not disorders.

Chapter Seven

LEARNING DISABILITIES & INTELLECTUAL DISABILITIES

LEARNING DISABILITIES

Learning Disability

A learning disability has nothing to do with intelligence. Great brains like Walt Disney and Winston Churchill, Einstein and Mozart (neither of whom spoke until he was 4 years old) had learning disabilities, along with about 4 million school-age kids and teens in the United States. You are not alone.

Learning disabilities are just a brain's wiring problems in receiving, processing, analyzing, or storing information.

Signs and Functions

There are many kinds of learning disorders that make it difficult for a student to learn.

- Some LDs make it difficult to focus, concentrate.

- Some LDs make it difficult for a student to read, write, spell, do math problems, solve space problems like geometry or parallel parking a car.

- Some LDs are social learning disabilities, difficulties in picking up the face, body, word cues that help us figure out someone else's mental state. There are many unwritten social rules based on the recognition of these cues that people with social learning disabilities miss— including the recognition of another person's point of view or personality, values, and interests.

- **Autism** is a term that describes a wide range of sensory, motor, language, social and emotional symptoms, with deficits in social interaction, communication, and repetitive, ritualistic behaviors. Difficulty with eye contact and impairment in relationships, communication, and how to handle social situations characterize autism. "Mindblindness," says Beverly Bowen, speech and language pathologist, "is the greatest social problem—difficulty in understanding someone else's feelings or point of view." Autism, and its milder variation, Asperger's disorder, are both characterized by problems with social interaction and communication. Young people with autism have difficulty communicating with, and appreciating the feelings of, others. Note: this disorder has nothing to do with intelligence. Many famous people, artists, writers, scientists like the brilliant animal behaviorist Dr. Temple Grandin, have autism. Autism is on a spectrum, from severe to mild, and thousands of people have some version of it, as many as one in ten schoolchildren, according to Hicks.

- **Dyslexia** is a verbal learning disorder which causes difficulties with both the written and spoken word, problems with both reading and writing. **Dyskinesia** is a disorder in voluntary movement, and the list of dysfunctions goes on.

- **ADHD** is a behavioral condition, not an intelligence problem. It is often associated with learning disabilities because people who have attention deficit disorder or attention hyperactivity deficit disorder often have trouble being still long enough to focus and study.

Detection of Signs and Symptoms

Learning disabilities show up as problems in speech, reading, writing, math, attention, in communicating with friends, parents, teachers, in following directions for work or games. Detecting signs and symptoms can be difficult, as kids get really good at covering up their problems.

There are children, teens, and even adults who know there is something wrong with them. But they have learned to navigate life successfully, though getting through school, work, relationships with friends and family is hard going for them. They are conscious of a missing piece, a glitch in the way they function. They just don't know why they are so good at what they're good at, and a disaster at something else.

My Intellectual/Learning Disability

Myself, I'm an excellent example of an assortment of intellectual and social disabilities. I can't parallel park a car. I have no spatial sense. I couldn't pass geometry. I got the second worst math SAT on the Eastern seacoast. I got one of the best scores and into a brilliant college for my English SAT. "We might as well let her out," said my kind high school math teacher. "She'll never pass math, but she's already been published."

I also don't pick up social cues, so people confuse and often frighten me. I blurt out what's on my mind, being without a mental social editor, so while I can very funny, I can also hurt people without meaning to. I'm told my manners at a party or any social gathering are strange, often abrupt. I wasn't diagnosed until adulthood, but when I was tested by a Yale psychologist, I was found to have math as well as spatial learning disabilities, and I have social disabilities. I came out a close relative of anyone on the Asperger's end of the autism spectrum. I have a really high IQ, I function fine in my writing and working life, but it's often hard, and socially I am odd. But, as I said, I am in good company.

Learning difficulties are just information-processing problems, but I know from experience as well as experts in brain science that the brain's neurological or biochemical disorders can be mistaken for intellectual disabilities or mental illness. Especially because learning problems are often accompanied by anxiety disorders. I mean, if your brain scrambles letters and can't figure a triangle from square, wouldn't you be anxious in a classroom? And if you have social learning disabilities and people scare you, wouldn't you be anxious in a classroom or at a party trying to fit in? I've had stomachaches, headaches, and panic attacks all my life from not fitting in. I've also had book awards, been published in thirteen languages, and I've taught writing classes all my life. I wouldn't change a thing.

In the past, when people had a learning disorder, they were grouped, without distinguishing their problems, with those who had mental illness or developmental delay, or intellectual disability. This kind of misdiagnosis is both terrifying and useless, as help and treatment, recovery or adjustment are then incorrect or impossible.

Confusion still exists today in the public's perception between:

1. Mental illness

2. Learning disabilities or disorders

3. Intellectual disabilities or what we used to call mental retardation

Intellectual Ability

Human intellectual abilities contain the following traits: abstract thought, communication, emotional intelligence, ability to learn, memory and knowledge, problem solution, teaching, reasoning, understanding, visual processing.

Many brain scientists agree that there are several, not just one type of intelligence.

- verbal or language IQ

- logical-mathematical IQ

- visual-spatial IQ

- bodily-kinesthetic IQ

- musical (aural) IQ

- intrapersonal IQ (philosophical, self-reflective, psychological)

- interpersonal IQ (sensitivity, understanding others, cooperative, communicative)
- existential IQ (spiritual or religious connection to the universe) ability to contemplate phenomena or questions beyond sensory or intellectual data, as physicists, cosmologists, mathematicians, as religious teachers and philosophers do.

Learning Disability Defined

If there is a tested normal capacity for learning (in some if not all of the above areas) and yet a failure to actually learn—this is the major signal that there may be a learning disability. If there is a gap between intelligence test scores and achievement scores, between potential and performance—this gap indicates a learning disability. The *DSM* defines a learning disability as being when the individual's achievement on standardized tests in reading, mathematics, or written expression is well below that expected for age, schooling, and level of intelligence (IQ).

Causes of Learning Disabilities

Hannah Carlson says in her *Living with Disabilities* that learning disabilities (LDs) and nonverbal learning disabilities (NLDs) are not caused by bad parenting, poor teaching, or cultural differences, although these may have an effect on performance. They are due to organic, neurological causes in the brain, mistakes in the wiring. Causes may include prenatal maternal malnutrition, infectious diseases, smoking, alcohol or drug intake, birth problems that deprive the brain of enough oxygen, or, after birth, from fevers, blows, ac-

cidents, meningitis. Heredity may be a factor. Neurological factors, not IQ, are the source of LDs, NLDs, ADD, and ADHD.

INTELLECTUAL DISABILITIES

Intellectual disabilities are defined by intellectual and performance limitations.

Intellectual functioning, intelligence, refers to mental capacity, the ability to learn, reason, and solve problems. This is usually measured by IQ tests. An average IQ is defined as 100. People with lower IQ's, however many difficulties they have with intellectual learning, may be quite capable of taking care of themselves and interacting socially appropriately with others. About 2 out of a hundred children are diagnosed with intellectual disabilities. Their IQ scores range between 50 and 70. Statistics show they often lead happy and productive lives. *DSM* lists the following levels for diagnosis.

- **Mild Mental Retardation IQ level 50-70.** Educable in school to 6th grade level, as adults can achieve social and vocational skills enough, with guidance, for self-support.

- **Moderate Retardation IQ level 35-40 to 50-55.** Although they cannot much benefit from academic education, with training and supervision, they can learn skills to work in sheltered workshops and cope in community environments.

- **Severe Mental Retardation IQ level 20-25 to 35-40.** May learn to talk and self-care, can learn to read simple words and perform simple tasks in supervised surroundings.

● **Profound Mental Retardation IQ level below 20 or 25.** Many have neurological basis for their impairment in sensory-motor function. Highly structured environment and supervision will always be necessary to maintain or improve performance of simple tasks, communication, self-care.

Down's Syndrome

There can also be a genetic cause for mental retardation. People with Down's syndrome have a characteristically flat face and eyelid folds recognizable at birth There are also other head and facial differences characteristic of other accompanying forms of mental retardation.

Partial List of other Disorders
Associated with Mental Retardation

Prenatal: During Pregnancy

1. Chromosome disorders such as Down's Syndrome
2. Muscular disorders, eye disorders, craniofacial disorders, skeletal disorders
3. Metabolic disorders
4. Developmental disorders of brain formation such as spina bifida and hydrocephalus
5. Environmental influences such as malnutrition, drugs, maternal disease

Perinatal—during labor and delivery

1. Abnormal labor and delivery
2. Infections
3. Head trauma
4. Seizures, breathing disorders

Postnatal—after delivery, during child's lifetime
1. Head injuries (accidents, abuse)
2. Infections like meningitis
3. Degenerative disorders like Huntington's or Parkinson's Disease
4. Seizure disorders like epilepsy
5. Environmental deprivation such as isolation, malnutrition, lack of affection and care-taking, or lack of educational stimulus

Testing

When testing for IQ, care must be taken to account for culture, gender, and age differences. The Army discovered this three generations ago when farmers and factory workers had trouble passing standardized English tests and college graduates flunked mechanics and building skills.

The Army had to devise two different sets of tests for different groups of people. Ethnic and cultural backgrounds, as well as gender information differences must also be accounted for to measure actual intelligence.

Intellectual functioning refers to mental capacity for learning, reasoning, problem-solving.

Adaptive behavior functioning refers to conceptual skills such as language, literacy, money, time, and number concepts, self-direction. It refers to social skills, interpersonal skills, sense of responsibility, ability to follow rules, and so forth. It refers to the practical skills needed for personal care, work, safety, such as travel, money exchange, communication devices, scheduling time.

Learning

Learning begins at the beginning, not just in school. Even in the womb, a baby is learning to survive. Babies are born with capabilities—to hear noises and make them, to touch and need touch, to seek warmth and nourishment, to communicate their needs and feelings through crying, with cooing. At six months, a baby knows its name, at one year a baby responds to the world outside, to music and talk and the sight of a favorite toy or face. At one year, unless the baby is Einstein who didn't talk until he was four, most babies have said their first word, and are at least thinking about walking.

Pre-teen and teen learning is the most interesting and terrifying of all. A passion for new experiences, the joy of danger and risk-taking, a preference for the company of their peers over family—these are the fertile characteristics of the teen brain. An article in *National Geographic* on teen brains based on information from NIMH (National Institute for Mental Health) reminds us that: If it were not for teenagers, the human race would not have gotten to where it is today. It was teenagers, with their energy and daring, who left Africa and spread humanity over the world. Evolution has selected for teen energy and courage over thousands of years. Without it, nobody would ever leave the safety of home or the security of the familiar to move into new territory.

TWO STORIES
THE AGONY AND THE TRIUMPH OF TWO TEENAGERS WITH AUTISM

Songs of the Gorilla Nation: My Journey through Autism
by Dawn Prince-Hughes, Ph.D.

"Dawn's form of autism is the intellectually, but not neces-sarily socially higher-functioning form called Asperger's Syn-drome. She describes herself as a 'wild thing out of context as a child' growing up into a 'wild thing in context with a family of gorillas' who taught her how to be civilized. It was the hours, days, months, and years she spent observing and working with the gorilla family at Woodland Park Zoo in Seattle that led not only to her professorship of anthropology, but her eventual ability to be a life partner and mother.

She still gets overloaded from too much outside stimula-tion—too many people, too many voices, too much activity and sound and sights—and she still has problems interacting with people. She still jumps when anyone touches her unex-pectedly. She still goes on and on about subjects that inter-est her without necessarily taking someone else's interests or views into account. But with a proper diagnosis, therapy, and practice, Dawn has learned coping strategies that have led her far away from the nightmare of her teens.

"I found it increasingly difficult to cope with the abuse at school and the rigidity—both academic and moral...I stood out as a freak: my tics, my monologues, my sensitivities, my imperviousness to criticism and suspicion of authority, my dis-dain for connection and avoidance of social interaction...my obsessions...my odd style of dressing and speaking all led to total ostracism and active aggression....

People would corner me in the bathroom and force my head into the toilet, slam me into my locker, and throw trash at me in the hall. They hit me in the head with books...took my food away...hung a sign with a derogatory word on it around my neck...I was swimming in a sea of ugliness, hate and intolerance...."

Dawn Prince-Hughes showed them all. With persistence, courage, and the informed diagnosis that her misfiring brain had nothing to do with her intellectual capacity, she attained not only her Ph.D. and professorship, but an honored place in her profession and a rich personal life.

Living well is the best revenge.**"**

Unwritten Rules of Social Relationships
Decoding Social Mysteries through
the Unique Perspectives of Autism
by Dr. Temple Grandin and Sean Barron

"Temple has classic autism. She was nonverbal until she was four. She had tantrums and meltdowns mostly because her receptors were hypersensitive to the stimulation of light, touch, and sound. She could not function socially because she could not read social cues or pick up emotional signals. Her impairment was so severe, institutionalization was recommended. Her mother refused to consider such a future for Temple. She had Temple diagnosed and organized experts to teach Temple how to function in the world through Temple's great strength—her intellect.

Subtle emotions are beyond her, she says. She thinks in pictures and learns solely through her intellect and visualization skills. She searches through her picture-memory archives for the right way to function in different social situations. And for her own calming comfort, Temple built what she calls her squeeze machine. She had become, among other areas of animal expertise, an expert in cattle handling, and she based the squeeze machine on the one she designed to calm cattle before slaughter. Temple Grandin is a genius, not only in understanding domestic animals, but in understanding and teaching about the problems of autism.

High school years, Temple reports in her book, were the worst years of her life. As long as other kids were fascinated, as she was, in science projects and building things, she had learned enough by rote to function socially. But as soon as girls' major interests shifted to bonding with each other, and things like clothes, hair, and makeup and dating boys, social life was over for Temple. To her those topics were silly and uninteresting.

For her social awkwardness, her fixations on horses and science topics in conversation, her disinterest in dating, her general oddness socially, she was teased and tormented. They called her names like 'Tape Recorder' and worse. Temple exploded with temper tantrums. Her mother responded by taking her out of school and enrolling her in a special boarding school for gifted, emotionally disturbed children.

Dr. Temple Grandin is, today, an internationally known animal scientist, which is what she wanted to be. Author of *Animals in Translation*, a ground breaking work about the way animals think, she is an expert on her beloved animal husbandry. She is, as well, a traveling lecturer and expert on the subject of autism. Her *Thinking in Pictures* transformed the world's perception of autism spectrum disorders. She presents the specific kind of social deficit typical of kids with autism—the difficulty in developing a 'theory of mind'—an ability to perceive that other people have thoughts, perceptions, and feelings different from their own.

But—living well is the best revenge and Temple Grandin lives well. 〟

Chapter Eight

TREATMENTS
AND RELAPSE
PREVENTION

Talk And Behavioral Therapies, Psychiatric Medications, Support Groups

You really don't want to walk around for the rest of your life with an untreated mental illness. Or an anxiety, personality, or behavioral disorder. Or an addiction or learning disability. It's too painful. Why suffer if you can find help to fix it, or at least stop some of the pain?

On the other hand, as Ray Fisher says in his *Unpublished Works*, you don't want so much therapy—or medication—so that you stop behaving at all. There are people who spend so much time in therapy that they never ultimately live their lives on their own.

Consult a Professional

Sharing anxiety or depression, a suspicion that you are addicted to alcohol or other drugs with your best friend is comforting. But a hug is not going to make the problem go away. You need a professional for an informed diagnosis, and to provide appropriate psychotherapy and, if necessary, medication. So, if you experience mental health problems, consult a professional.

Professional Treatment, Therapy, and Medication

Much of the following information is taken from Hannah Carlson's book *The Courage to Lead: Start Your Own Support Group—Mental Illnesses and Addictions*.

The type and amount of professional treatment for mental illnesses from psychotic disorders to major depression, from addictive to personality disorders, varies depending on the severity of the illness, the coping skills of the person involved, the family and environmental supports available, and the community resources.

Treatment is often provided by a team of professionals that may include a psychologist or psychiatrist, psychiatric nurse, social worker, rehabilitation worker, case manager, and vocational counselor.

Therapy and Training

- **Psychotherapy.** In addition to providing support and empathy, therapy should include assistance in the development of self-awareness, an understanding of moods and their management, and an education about the particular symptoms of the illness as well the impact on relationships, work, and the ability to solve problems and use good judgment. The purpose of good therapy is to help people with disorders find and use their own insights and skills in their lives. Psychotherapy can be provided in groups, individually, or both, whatever produces the best results. Some people benefit from the experience of others in group therapy, some need more individual focus until they are able to understand their illness and are able to relate to others.

- **Behavioral therapy.** Behavioral therapists identify behaviors that interfere with healthy and productive responses to the demands of life. Behaviors are everything we do, think, and feel. New behaviors are developed to replace dysfunctional or maladaptive behaviors. Changing behavior has been found by researchers to change the brain's chemistry, its neuronal circuitry, and therefore, how we think and feel. Behavioral therapy teaches new, more effective coping skills and behaviors. There are many types of behavioral therapy such as exposure and response prevention used to treat obsessive-compulsive disorders and some impulse control disorders, and play therapy which is effective with children who are given toys to express themselves as well as to create role models to work out the desired solution.

- **Cognitive behavioral therapy (CBT)** is based in dialogue, in talks with the therapist. The therapist's job is to help develop not only new behavioral skills, but insight into the causative factors of inappropriate or ineffective behaviors. The purpose is to change the cognitive, the thinking structure, the feeling structure, all the misunderstandings about life and relationships that create fear and anxiety and destructive coping behaviors.

● **Rehabilitative therapy** identifies strengths and weaknesses in the ability to negotiate the demands of work, home, school, and community living. Strategies and assistive aids are developed to help minimize the impact of the disability in coping with everyday life. These include social skills training, cognitive remediation (attention, concentration, problem solving, memory, planning, organizing, and decision-making training), impulsive control and other behavior modification. This therapy may also include learning new strategies for ways to think and act, with friends, parents, teachers.

Assistive aids can include planners/organizers, desired behavior checklists/reminders, watches with beepers, reminder memos posted near frequently used places such as the telephone, front door, bathroom mirror, in the car.

● **Hospitalization** is recommended for those episodes in the course of a mental illness when there is actual or potential threat of danger to one's self or others. There may be abuse or neglect of the self (inadequate daily hygiene, food, clothing) resulting in a risk of disease, illness, injury, or life-threatening malnutrition. There may be danger to others if violence is indicated as a component of the mental illness or disorder.

Most hospitalizations last seventy-two hours, for stabilization. If there is a risk of harming the self or others, the director of the hospital, treating psychiatrist, or family members may petition for and may be granted a court order, so that people can be held against their will for a longer commitment of time. Some people visit psychiatric hospitals once. Others need to revisit for intermittent care when symptoms resurface.

When seeking a diagnosis and treatment, second, even third opinions are desirable. Investigate the diagnosis and treatment recommendations in order to obtain the treatment that provides the most improvement and fastest restoration to mental health.

- **Alternative interventions.** Holistic medicine and natural remedies have been employed by healers for thousands of years before psychotherapy and psychopharmacology became the treatments of choice. Some of the most commonly sought-after interventions include: acupuncture and acupressure, homeopathy, and Ayurvedic traditions which employ principles and techniques derived from ancient China, India, and the native people of many different countries. These healing disciplines base their practices of medicine on liberating and cleansing the flow of life forces of energy within each person. In Chinese medicine, the energy is called ch'i. In Ayurvedic medicine, it is referred to as prana.

● **Nutrition and herbal supplements** such as Lecithin, inositol, and St. John's Wort are as widely accepted and help to relieve depression, anxiety, and some side-effects of medications. Gingko biloba is taken by some to relieve the sexual impairment experienced as a side-effect to anti-depressant medications. Echinacea purpurea, Goldenseal, Bitter melon are among the many the herbal remedies available to address restlessness and other side-effects. Taking a multi-vitamin, multi-mineral tablet each day helps to restore some of the vitamins and minerals lost due to prescribed medications, such as the vitamin A and vitamin B complex. Vitamin E has been shown to help counteract the tardive dyskinesia symptoms (involuntary movements) resulting from some medications. Studies are not conclusive that vitamin, mineral, and herbal supplements effect relief. None are sufficient as a replacement for prescription medication when medication is recommended or psychotherapy.

Medications

There are many medications currently prescribed to treat various mental illnesses. The most frequently prescribed include anti-psychotics and antidepressants. These classes of drugs seem to be effective in treating the symptoms of schizophrenia and other psychotic disorders, depression, anxiety and some symptoms of personality disorders and mood disorders.

Psychotropic medications are categorized by their structures and activities in the brain. Simply put, SSRIs (selective serotonin reuptake inhibitors) such as Prozac, Luvox, Zoloft, and Paxil prevent the brain's nerve cells from disposing of the neurotransmitter serotonin. These medications are commonly prescribed for depression and anxiety.

MAO inhibitors (monoamine oxidase) such as Marplan, Parnate, and Nardil, it is hypothesized, increase the serotonin, dopamine, and norepinephrine neurotransmitter levels by inhibiting the metabolizing enzyme that normally breaks down neurotransmitters, and are thought to work by increasing the levels of serotonin and norepinephrine.

Benzodiazepines such as Valium, Klonopin, Librium, Ativan, Centrax and Xanax enhance the activity of GABA (gamma-aminobutyric acid), a neurotransmitter that inhibits transmissions. They are effective in treating anxiety, but can be addictive and difficult to stop taking.

Tricyclic antidepressants such as Anafranil, Elavil, and Tofranil block norepinephrine and serotonin to achieve a similar affect as the SSRIs. They are prescribed for OCD, panic, depression, eating disorders, and chronic pain.

Anti-psychotics, also known as neuroleptics, lower the level of the neurotransmitter dopamine. Commonly prescribed anti-psychotic medications used to treat schizophrenia and other psychotic disorders include: Risperdol, Thorazine, Mellaril, Prolixin, Stelazine, Haldol, and Clozaril.

Commonly prescribed medications used for bipolar disorder include anti-spasmodics which increase GABA levels such as Tegretol, and Depakote. Lithium, also used, is considered an effective drug for bipolar disorder, and can be used to prevent recurring episodes of depression.

There are new breakthroughs in medication for mental health disorders all the time. Now that MRI is available, we can actually see how medication works and make adjustments.

Side-effects

As with all medications, there is the possibility of side-effects when taking psychotropic medication. These side-effects can often be almost as difficult to live with as the mental illness. The effects can vary from mild to severe. In some cases, the side-effects disappear after a few weeks of taking the medications. In other cases, the side-effects never go away. In some extreme cases, the side-effects themselves become a second illness such as an addiction to Valium, or the acquiring of tardive dyskinesia, involuntary spasm of facial and body muscles, as a result of long-term taking some anti-psychotic mediation. Because of the possible effects of these medications, they should only be taken under supervision.

Some frequently reported side-effects include: excessive tiredness, headaches, heartburn/stomach aches, dry mouth, blurred speech or vision, seizures, constipation, stiffness, tremors, jumpiness or restlessness, hyperactivity, excessive weight gain or loss, impaired sexual functioning, seizures, hypersensitivity to light, liver damage, and eye damage.

In rare individuals, some medications can produce the opposite of what they were prescribed for. For example, an antidepressant may increase the impulse to commit suicide. Discuss with your doctor any desire to give up a medication. There may be side effects, and these can be monitored.

The Decision to Medicate

The decision to medicate is not a simple one. Medication can sometimes cure mental illness. Often, it just masks or reduces the symptoms to a tolerable level.

Prescribing psychotropic medications is highly specialized. For this reason, it is best that a fully experienced psychiatrist rather than a general physician be consulted. Prescribing physicians who are not familiar with the medication usually follow the manufacturer's recommended dosage. This means it could take several months before the right medication or dosage level is achieved to effectively address the symptoms according to the rate of the individual's metabolism. Side effects must be explained, understood, perhaps even compensated for. Once the optimum medication and dosage have been achieved, the benefits of freedom from sometimes physically painful mental distress can be well worth waiting out the period of adjustment.

The most commonly prescribed antidepressants in 2010 were Zoloft, Celexa, Prozac, Lexapro, Cymbalta, and Paxil.

The side-effects of medications can be mitigated or reduced by adding other medications, through supplements such as herbal remedies, and by altering diet. Some side-effects are significant enough that a person will choose to suffer the symptoms of the illness rather than the side-effects of the medication. For example, some teenage boys and men who suffer from the impairment of sexual function find that this side-effect contributes to their symptoms of depression and therefore stop taking the medication for that reason alone. Some older teenage girls and women who are pregnant or nursing stop taking the medication and risk the return of their symptoms rather than worry about the potential effects of the medication on the baby.

Support Groups

If you go online, or check the listings at the back of this book, you will find lists of support groups to join for every age, for every illness, for every addiction.

People of every age from preteens to teens to young adults to full adults have discovered that sharing the experience of their pain, strength, and tools for recovery makes them all stronger, makes them feel no longer alone in their struggle to live life as normally as the normal.

Talking to others in the same boat provides community and instant friendship. You discover you are no longer alone.

In the end we all want freedom from the pain of psychological suffering. This can only happen when the ways of the self and its fears and desires are understood, whether that self comes from a brain that is ordinary, unordinary, or extraordinary. This sharing, this pooling of information, energy, and self-exploration, this understanding of the ways of your self, is the basis of the dialogues in the support groups. You will be helped to recover, and then help others, pay it forward, pass it on.

My favorite quote from the great writer, poet, and teacher Maya Angelou says, is:

"When you get, give
When you learn, teach."

STORY
TEEN IN A WHEELCHAIR

❝I sit in my wheelchair. Always something hurts somewhere, pressure sores on my behind, muscle cramp, the kind of headache you get from being angry at other people's dumb remarks. But it's all right with me. I'm glad I'm still alive. I shouldn't be.

I have cerebral palsy, meaning, in my case, because I was damaged while I was being born, I have no control over my movements and I spaz all the time. I look like a crazy puppet flailing in the wind unless my arms and legs are strapped or I'm feeling really relaxed. If I'm really upset, my face twitches, too. I know all this because a) I've seen myself in mirrors, and b) I've kicked and swatted people who come near me to feed, change, get me in and out of my chair to bed or to shower. I'm completely helpless. This makes me feel angry and depressed sometimes. I'm told I'm charming and good-looking, so despite my helplessness, I have made good friends among group home staff and volunteers who make me feel glad I'm here.

And then there are the others, the ones who tell everybody my story as if I were a zoo exhibit. I can't speak, but I can hear really well. They think because I can't speak, because I can only make ugly sounds, grunts and howls, that I don't understand all I hear. Because I can't speak, they don't know what I know, how much I know. They think I'm mentally retarded, although it's more politically correct to say that, besides cerebral palsy, I have intellectual disabilities. I'm not so sure. My father left the minute he heard my diagnosis when I was a baby. My mother died when I was five of alcoholism. I grew up

in an institution where we spent our days lined up against a wall. I think maybe I just haven't been taught enough. Because of malnutrition in the institution, I have cystic fibrosis.

Now I live in a group home with especially trained staff to care for me. I have enough to eat, unlike the institution days, and I'm warm. I get therapy. I even have what they call an assisted job in a greenhouse. It's true staff has to help me with this, and everything else just to stay alive. I can communicate 'yes' and 'no' with my eyes and eyebrows (open wide, raise eyebrows for yes, look down, lower eyebrows for no), but I have no control over any other muscles. I have to be bathed, dressed, fed, put to bed at night like a baby. I live in my chair. I am usually consulted about where I want to be pushed.

On weekends, I'm off in my staff-driven van for shopping. Last Saturday, while I was helped to help push the cart down the frozen food aisle, I heard a woman say, 'Wish I was that kid. Don't they have it easy, sitting in a chair all day?'**"**

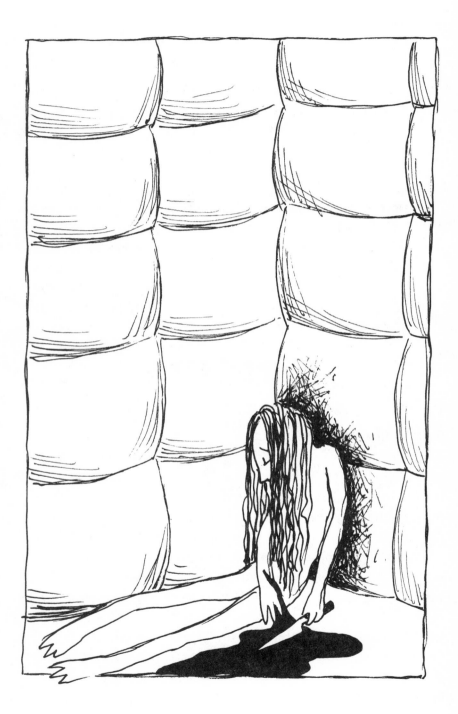

Chapter Nine

SUICIDE

We're Killing Ourselves

The courage to live in the face of how hard life is, and the risks we take for ourselves and others, has always been a mystery to me. But life is extraordinary in its persistence, and young people are the most courageous of all. The issue of living, and how to deal with its pain, is the issue of most philosophies, religions, and this book.

But enough young people *do* commit suicide to let us know something really is wrong with how our species lives and brings up its young. According to the YRBS (Youth Risk Behavior Survey) of the CDC (Centers for Disease Control), by 2002, suicide in the United States was the third leading cause of death among youth. Only accidents and homicide kill more young people, and among college students, only accidental injury kills more young people than suicide.

Suggested causes for the higher rate of suicide in the United States in the last half century range from the increased rate of depression since the 1950s to the increased availability of firearms and drugs. Psychiatrists point to the lack of family cohesion, or to the 1960s revolution in psychosexual relationships among the young that include greater expectations and so greater disappointments. A greater use of drugs and alcohol among the young during that period affected both suicide and accidental deaths.

Males have a higher rate of suicide than females, contrary to the belief that females are the more emotionally unstable gender. But it is suggested that the reason for this is that males more often use lethal weapons like guns and so have a greater success rate.

Some Interesting Facts about Suicide

- Altogether, about 4,000 young people aged 15-24 died by suicide in the year 2002. The rate has declined slightly. This is thought by some experts to be due to the increased use of antidepressant medications in treating young depressed people.

- Youth not currently in school, in CDC studies, are at higher risk than those who are in school.

- Suicidal patterns vary not only among males and females but among different ethnic groups. In 2002, young Native Americans and Alaskan Natives had the highest rates at 17.9 per 100,000, then whites at 10.6, 6.6 for Hispanic youth, 6.5 for African-American youth, 5.3 for Asian Americans/Pacific Islanders.

- In view of these extremely high figures, the National Strategy for Suicide Prevention developed by the Department of Health and Human Services has increased its attention to youth suicide.

· ·

Risk Factors for Suicide in Teens and Young Adults

Adapted from Dr. Herbert Hendin's section on Youth Suicide in *Treating and Preventing Adolescent Mental Health Disorders.*

1. **Psychopathology/Mental Illness**
   Depression; Drug and alcohol abuse / gambling / compulsive spending; Aggressive-impulse behavior; Hopelessness / pessimism / feelings of not belonging; Conduct disorder (mostly male); Panic disorder (mostly female)

2. **Family and Genetic**
   Family history of suicidal behavior; Parental psychopathology

3. **Environment**
   Firearm, drug availability; Broken family, lack of family cohesion; Lack of family / parental support; Parent-child conflict; Difficult life events: death; bullying (for size, sexual orientation, mental problems, color, class, money—whatever); relocation, etc.; Child sex abuse; Suicide contagion, previous suicide attempts

4. **Brain Neurobiochemical Dysfunction**

· ·

Prevention

The causes of suicide are many and varied. And because so many overlapping causes may occur at the same time, suicide prevention is a delicate and difficult issue. There are screening tests, there are hotlines, there are crisis centers. But none of these will work if you don't speak up!

● Speak up if you go through a really long, dark mood of depression so intense you think maybe life isn't worth the struggle and consider it might be easier just to end it all.

● Speak up if a friend complains too long of black moods. These can manifest as periods of dark despair, talking about life as if it weren't worth living, as if there was nothing to live for.

Suicide prevention is a collective effort. We have to listen to each other, especially when one of us falls down that deep, dark well of loneliness, inner pain, and the hopeless desperation of suicidal ideas.

Treatment

● **Screening.** There are screening tests and self-report questionnaires given by health services that the U.S. Surgeon General suggests are especially helpful in suicide prevention among children, teens, and young adults. These must be followed up by clinical interviews for clarity.

- **Medical.** Full medical evaluation to evaluate whether low thyroid, malnutrition, physical illness, or other medical cause underlies the suicidal depression. This includes alcohol and drug abuse.

- **Drug therapy.** Psychotropic medication may be prescribed such as that used for anxiety, depression, bipolar cycling, or self-harm behaviors.

- **Temporary hospitalization** may reduce the danger of harming oneself or others.

- **Talk therapy.** Cognitive Behavior Talk therapy (CBT) for Suicide Prevention in combination with anti-depression or anti-anxiety medication has been shown to reduce suicidal thinking in teens.

As always, sharing the burden, the confusion, and survival tools with someone else reduces the loneliness of pain.

Youth Suicide Prevention Programs

There are school, college, and community programs that provide ongoing support and information for suicidal young people and their families. Dial information for your local group telephone number, a suicide hotline, or 911.

Programs that educate students about suicide can increase students' knowledge of mental illness and suicide, external environment and suicide, neurobiological abnormalities and suicide, family history and behavior and suicide, personal social skills, dropping out of school, and other psychosocial problems that influence suicidal behavior, and provide help-seeking information.

Programs that educate teachers, counselors, parents and community gate-keepers increase prevention. These programs may include screening tests for youth at risk and the underlying disorders.

Source of and Cure for Psychological Suffering

The source of psychological suffering, we have learned, is ourselves. And so, therefore, is the cure.

Think about this. For 4 billion years, life was shaped by nature—evolution and natural selection of the fittest to survive. Then, about 4 million years ago, the human species began to evolve, and *the human brain, with its tools and eventually its technology from sharpened rock to biological engineering, became the force that most shaped and continues to shape life on Earth.*

Along with our technological understanding, we must also use our psychological understanding, our insight. If we could make human society less painful for ourselves and each other, we might make it less inviting to want out. And we have the capability—we can do this.

STORY
I WANT OUT

"I'm in the bathroom. I have locked the door. The bathtub is already half full of the hottest water I can stand. The fresh blade is on the edge of the sink. I have been staring into the tall bathroom mirror for a long time. I'm not sure why. Am I checking my makeup, my new black camisole top, the fall of my long hair, to make sure that, when they find me, I look right?

Am I saying goodbye to the person I have been staring at in this mirror for fifteen years?

I have already swallowed the pills, the pain-killers, from the bottle in my mother's bathroom. I've swallowed enough pills to overdose, I'm pretty sure, but I am going to cut my wrists and bleed out in the bathtub to make absolutely sure. I've watched enough scenes like this on *Law and Order; SVU* to know how it's done, how to make the cuts, I mean. I've taken enough pills to put me at least to sleep, so if the pills and cuts don't kill me, hopefully at least I'll slide under the water and drown.

Is this overkill? Or am I just making a bad joke.

You'll be asking why I'm doing this. Even *I'm* still asking why I'm doing this.

For *attention*! For at long last so that someone in this family pays attention to me. To *me*! Not to my sister—to me!

"You're not the problem, dear," says my mother, when I ask why every dinner conversation, every argument in the library where my parents drink before dinner every evening, every after-dinner or late-night scene with my mother trailing around the apartment in her long, white Dracula-wardrobe nightgowns is about my sister, never me.

I'm the good girl, get it? My sister is the bad girl. She's brilliant in school, although she's always on probation for breaking rules (my grades are average, and I'm never in trouble), she's a major talent at ballet school (even though I'm the one who wants to be a dancer), she's good at sports even if she despises them as a waste of her writing time, she's popular (even if all she cares about is being by herself to read her million books).

She sneaks out late at night to meet boys or her friends and bribes the doorman not to tell (I wouldn't dare, although she's invited me to tag along).

Who would have thought the bad girl would get every particle of attention? It's like she sucks up all the oxygen in this family.

But while I'm making jokes about this, I'm so depressed all the time I can hardly breathe. I feel invisible. It's not that I want to be yelled at the way my sister gets yelled at for everything she says and does. And I really don't envy her all that punishment. But I keep wanting to scream, "I'm here, too. Look at me, too."

I've tried this before, this cutting myself. Obviously, it didn't work. I hardly even got scolded for the mess.

Will it work this time? Will it work now?

And will I know, finally, that attention has been paid?**"**

Chapter Ten

RECOVERY
Responsibility For Treatment, Informed Behavior, Meditation, And Exercise

What Is Recovery?

Being in recovery for mental illness, learning disabilities, intellectual disabilities, or addictions lessens the suffering and improves skills in living life. Therapy does not necessarily mean cure. It's not like having a broken arm that can be completely recovered if it is set properly by a good doctor. Neither surgery nor neuroscience, not talk or behavioral therapy or even psychotropic drugs can create a perfectly functioning brain out of an imperfectly wired brain. Cures may or may not happen, but at least treatment and self-understanding lessen the suffering.

There Is No Stigma Attached to Labels

There are things the matter with all of us. Those with labels are the lucky ones. As a matter of fact, a new *DSM* (*DSM*-V) has added and subtracted a few more labels and classifications. It has been discovered how to help most of those groups. But the rest of humanity has to suffer and deal with what's wrong with them.

The human brain is the most complex thing we have yet discovered in the universe, and while all brains are overall pretty much alike, as snowflakes are, like snowflakes they are all slightly different and all are to some extent imperfectly wired. That means we are all faulty and always in recovery from our mistaken perceptions and behavior. Just having a human brain distorts reality and the perception of the universe. The brain contains not necessarily useful memories of our evolutionary history back to the ameba. It inputs, not necessarily accurately, what our five senses pick up, plus a particular, biased cultural education, plus personal experiences which are edited and re-edited versions of our memories.

Our brains are also affected by various organs and chemicals, by our physical health, by exposure to environment and other people. And we call this hodge-podge of chemistry, self-protective survival skills, thoughts, feelings, and memories the 'truth'.

The real truth is, a lot of what goes on in the human brain is more like a confusion of the fears and aching desires going on in every human head than truth—the truth being what is actually going on in our lives and in our physical universe. Most of us spend our lives trying to escape our human suffering. We want to take our minds off our problems with drugs or digital entertainment, shopping or gambling or whatever, rather than seeking the truth of what is really, actually going on with being a human being in relationship to a universe we do not yet fully understand. It's scary out there. It unbalances us all, with or without labels. It leaves all human beings in continual recovery from just having a self-conscious human brain that can remember and mourn or imitate the past, and project and fear the future.

This leaves us all in recovery just from the shocks human brains are susceptible to, from the stories we tell ourselves about what's going on in our lives and what we think is going to go on.

None of Us Ever Wholly Recovers from the Shock of Being Human: We Are All Always Psychologically in Recovery.

Teens at Risk

It's difficult to be a human being. Their parents and teachers and other adults may have buried this fact, but teens and young adults know this. It's why so many are at risk for suicide. And it's why, if teens can make it through the fears of adolescence, they often bury themselves alive, as so many of the previous generations did before them, in the safety of inherited patterns of life, in work, in the form of marriage, money, possessions, and position. Living can be so frightening, we numb out with the boredom of repetition rather than risk bad feelings or bullying for being different. It takes courage to be aware and awake, to grow up and mature through all the stages of life. And if this courage can begin in the teen years, you're ahead of the game.

We Are All Responsible for Ourselves

The responsibility for the perception of problems, getting diagnosis, seeking help, and continuing recovery is always ultimately our own. Even a young child screams out when it is wet, cold, hungry, lonely, or unhappy in an effort for diagnosis and help in recovering from whatever is wrong.

If children holler out when they are unhappy until they get help, we can, too. The responsibility is ours, and the older we get, the more we take over from adults, learn to take care of ourselves, and *then help the next one in pain.*

Informed Behavior

Therapy isn't enough. Psychotropic medication isn't enough. With information and meds, if they are prescribed, the ongoing task throughout all our lives is **to see our behavior and change it, which in itself will rewire the brain.**

We are responsible, therefore, not only to seek help, but to take the ball, run with it, and pass it forward.

There are people who enjoy being perpetual patients. Like children, they just want to be taken care of all their lives,

I have a technical word for that. *Yuck.*

My father, who was a physician, used to say to me, "Don't ever develop a cripple's mentality—*even if you are mentally or physically crippled.* Once you've gotten the help you need, keep on carrying on, so you and everyone else can help the next guy."

Our Original Mistake

Our human brain made an original evolutionary mistake in our understanding of the outer world. Without modern technology, our eyes could not see that the physical universe was made of energy, waves, and particles, not solid objects. We saw boundaries around everything, and decided that everything was separate from everything and everyone else. It gave us the idea that each of us is alone under the stars, and the idea made us feel lonely. It's true we each live inside our own skins. But those skins are porous. Physics reminds us that everything is made of particles and hangs out together in a universe without boundaries.

We really are all in this thing we call life together. Can we see there is really no separation? Can we act this way—knowing that every part, every thought, every action affects the whole universe?

Meditation and Exercise

Meditation is an interesting word. It does not mean standing on your head in a corner muttering strange words in a foreign language. It simply means to pay attention. It's important to stress that paying attention means to *look at actions, thoughts, feelings, the world with new eyes, not through the screen of old memories—and not through the screen of old judgments, old fears, yesterday's desires.*

Can we look at each other, at ourselves, at what we're doing and feeling as if for the first time, each time? Everything changes. Can we keep up by paying constant, actual attention?

Important Aspects of Meditation

- Pay attention (observe, don't judge) to your thoughts and feelings as often as you can throughout your day. Don't live automatically. *Get to know and understand yourself so you can change what you want to change.*

- To take an hour, half an hour, a few minutes if that's all you can do at first to quiet your brain and body so you *can* meditate. This means to listen to what you are thinking and feeling—again, so you get to know yourself and your reactions and can change what you want to change, stop what you want to stop.

- There are many meditative practices from chanting to mantras, from breath-counting to yoga, dance, martial arts forms, to just long, quiet (no iPod) walks for those who have trouble sitting still. For some people, reading meditation books like the Bible, books by the philosopher Krishnamurti, the teachings of the Buddha or Jesus, the meditations of Lao Tzu, the Hindu Gita, the poems of Maya Angelou. *Again, the whole point is to listen to your own self, your thoughts and feelings.*

- Breathing practice and other relaxation techniques help some people.

The reason for meditation and mindful exercise is to let go of your daily busyness and pay attention to what is going on in-side you. This attention tells you about your self—oh, there's *that* again. *And then let it go!* Meditation, connecting with the universe and turning your life over to its care, works better as a high than turning into stoners and drinkers. The author has done them all and can vouch personally for this. As someone with bipolar disorder and assorted addictions, meditation has helped along with meds to calm my anxieties and manic cycling of moods, release me from cravings, and allowed my intelligence to say to myself, "go this way, not that." And to be part of everything and everyone, not lonely and separate.

Meditation is not just a spiritual practice, it's an extremely practical practice. It's the way to use your own mind to heal and help yourself, see for yourself that your thoughts and feelings do not have to dictate your life. You can watch them, let them pass, and then do the healthy thing—react to the outer, not the inner world.

Use Your Strengths to Offset Your Weaknesses

You can learn your strengths as well as your weaknesses in meditation, in paying attention to your thoughts, feelings, and behaviors, in all the relationships to the people and activities of your daily life. You may have all kinds of strengths you aren't aware of, like humor, tolerance, patience. If you don't have intuitive understanding of other people, you may be able to compensate by developing a good memory for social conventions. If you have too quick a temper, you may be able to learn to leave space before you respond. If you suffer depression, you may be able to learn it will pass even if it doesn't feel that way, and not destroy yourself in the meantime. There are ways, like physical exercise, to temporarily improve your mood. Knowing you have strengths to get through things goes a long way when times are bad for you. There are tools for living better than you feel. You just need to develop strong psychological muscles as well as physical ones.

Get Help to Find Your Strengths as Well as to Diagnose Weaknesses

If you need help, or an extra mirror through someone else's eyes, in objectively seeing yourself (and we all do!), ask a friend, a teacher you trust, a counselor or therapist to help you look at yourself and the way you are living your daily life. Family may be too close, too involved, too caring, too threatened or too threatening, to offer clear and objective mirroring.

Keep a daily watch over the weak or difficult or flawed thoughts, feelings, or behaviors, any shadows cast by mental illness, personality or behavioral disorder, or addiction.

The watching, the looking itself will create mentally healthy changes in your brain's wiring.

The talking over and hearing an objective, intelligent point of view will influence mentally healthy changes in behavior. And check what you are doing with a trusted advisor, so you know you are on track instead of just wandering.

Books by intelligent teachers and philosophers are excellent mirrors for examining and changing your own attitudes and behavior. As you would use a crutch, wheelchair, or cane for a broken foot until you can walk on your own, use the mirror of other eyes until you can see your own life with new eyes instead of old.

TRAUMATIC BRAIN INJURY: A METAPHOR
FOR PAYING ATTENTION/MEDITATION

"No matter what happens to me now, I'm glad to be alive. I didn't used to care. Now I do. I'm not sure why. This glad- to- be- alive happiness may be part of my brain injury. My brain has forgotten the fears and angers I used to have, along with most of the old movies I've seen, and a lot of old memories — all are gone with the wind or whatever it was that battered my head.

I'm not sure why, and it has been explained to me, neither do the brain surgeons. I got beaten up badly on the top floor of a parking garage. My right brain was so battered, the surgeon had to take a chunk out. I should not have survived either the head injury or the surgery. The same was true of the other guys on the same hospital floor. They had lived through motorcycle or car accidents, sports moves or falls that went wrong, street fights and beatings. Some of them wished they hadn't — lived through it, I mean.

Head injuries, when the brain gets bruised or shaken, are not like breaking a bone in the rest of the body. Bones properly set can heal pretty quickly as good as new, surgeons and therapists tell me. But brain tissue, nerve tissue, takes a long time to heal, and may never fully recover. The doctors also told me and my parents that there might be differences in me, changes in my personality that would never entirely go away.

So far, my girlfriend tells me, this has turned out to be true. I don't any longer have to wear the protective helmet I wore in rehab — I'd lost my sense of balance and I kept falling down. I don't have to sleep under a net — I kept trying to get out of bed even if I couldn't. But she says I'm not the same person I was. She says I'm nicer. She says I'm more loving. She says I never stop talking.

What I know is that it's constantly hard work now to try to repair my own brain. I've forgotten a lot of words, the names of things among other memories. Just to stay in touch with reality, to see myself in relationship to what's going on is hard, never mind the word for my cell phone or my laptop or my pants.

I think I need new software. Sometimes I think everybody does, actually, because doesn't reality keep changing for us all? I mean, nothing stays the same for anyone, does it.

I've been warned about the stages of recovery for traumatic brain injury.

1. **Confusion and agitation.** It was scary and it felt as if it would never end. I don't know if it's ended for me or I've just gotten used to the confusion. But now it feels funny to me instead of scary, this thing about so much being new to me. Some guys on my floor got angry. Their change of personality scared everybody.

2. **Denial.** You go through a phase of feeling better and stronger physically, even if, once they let you go home, you put your shoes in the fridge and the ice cream under the bed. I kept insisting I could drive when I was still walking into walls. Apparently, there are two types of denial. One is an emotional one. Something has happened that is so terrible, so terrifying, you don't want to deal with it. The second type comes from the

brain injury physically—your brain just can't process certain kinds of information anymore.

3. **Anger and depression.** Not all of these are because of the brain injury and chemical changes in the brain. I went from anger at myself for being in the wrong place at the wrong time, to anger at whoever beat me up, to life in general for being unfair. Anger alternated with depression and self-pity—that why-me stuff.

4. **Testing.** Once I got out of the hospital, I spent every day trying to do everything I ever did before—just taking a walk was a test of endurance, direction, and wondering if I got my clothes on right.

5. **Acceptance.** I keep being told I'm a different person. I feel different because a lot of my memory has begun to come back and I know I'm not the same. My hair has grown over the scars on my head, I'm back at school with my buddies and my girlfriend, and my outward life is pretty much what it was, even my stamina and physical strength. But I'm not the same person. I know this and so do other people. This is the part that's hard to accept, the no longer knowing who you are, the reassembling your self from one day to the next, with no idea what the future looks like or whether your brain will hold up or break down.**"**

Section Two

ANXIETY DISORDER

Self-Test Screening Questions

*Adapted from the Sheenan Test for Anxiety, ©Patty Fleener, M.S.W.
And the Anxiety Screening Test, ©Benjamin J. Sadock, M.D. and
Waguih William IsHak, M.D. New York University*

Please answer Yes, No, Sometimes to the following questions:

1. Do you feel that you worry
    excessively about many
    things?   ❑ Yes   ❑ No   ❑ Somtimes

2. Do you experience difficulty
    getting your breath, panting,
    over-breathing, dizziness?   ❑ Yes   ❑ No   ❑ Somtimes

3. Do you fear losing control
    of yourself, or of going
    insane?   ❑ Yes   ❑ No   ❑ Somtimes

4. Do you fear you are dying?
    Or something terrible is
    going to happen?   ❑ Yes   ❑ No   ❑ Somtimes

5. Do you have specific fears
    of certain things? Intruders?
    The dark? Being hurt?   ❑ Yes   ❑ No   ❑ Somtimes

6. Do you have sleep problems
    such as difficulty falling asleep,
    waking suddenly afraid
    in the middle of the night?   ❑ Yes   ❑ No   ❑ Somtimes

7. Do you avoid social or
   performance situations,
   even just leaving the house
   because of fear? ❑ Yes ❑ No ❑ Somtimes

8. Do you have unexpected
   depressions or mood swings
   with little or no provocation? ❑ Yes ❑ No ❑ Somtimes

9. Do you persistently relive
   unpleasant events from the past,
   worry they will reoccur? ❑ Yes ❑ No ❑ Somtimes

10. Do you worry overly about
    your health? About your
    popularity? About how you
    look? About everything from
    whether the doors are locked
    to the house catching fire?
    Do you have recurrent, persistent,
    unwanted thoughts? ❑ Yes ❑ No ❑ Somtimes

11. Do you have to repeat certain
    acts over and over again
    to feel safe, like rituals? ❑ Yes ❑ No ❑ Somtimes

RESULTS

The more you answered **YES** to these questions, the more serious your anxiety may be. Please consult with an informed adult,
a psychologist, physician, licensed mental health professional experienced in diagnosing and treating anxiety.

OBSESSIVE-COMPULSIVE DISORDER

OCD Screening Checklist

Copyright, J. H. Greist, J. W. Jefferson, I. M. Marks. American Psychiatric Press, 1986.

1. Do you have thoughts that bother you or make you anxious and that you can't get rid of regardless of how hard you try?

2. Do you have a tendency to keep things extremely clean or to wash your hands very frequently, more than other people you know?

3. Do you check things over and over to excess?

4. Do you have to straighten, order, or tidy things so much that it interferes with other things you want to do?

5. Do you worry excessively about acting or speaking more aggressively than you should?

6. Do you have great difficulty discarding things even when they have no practical value?

People with OCD usually have difficulty with some of the following activities. Answer each question by circling the appropriate number next to it.

0   No problem with activity—takes me same time as average person. I do not need to repeat or avoid it.

1 *Activity takes me twice as long as most people, or I have to repeat it twice, or I tend to avoid it.*

2 *Activity takes me three times as long as most people, or I have to repeat it three or more times, or I usually avoid it.*

Score	Activity
0 1 2	Taking a bath/shower
0 1 2	Washing dishes
0 1 2	Turning lights and taps on or off
0 1 2	Mailing letters
0 1 2	Form filing
0 1 2	Washing hands/face
0 1 2	Handling/cooking food
0 1 2	Locking or closing doors or windows
0 1 2	Reading
0 1 2	Care of hair (washing, combing, brushing)
0 1 2	Cleaning house
0 1 2	Using electrical appliances, heaters
0 1 2	Writing
0 1 2	Brushing teeth
0 1 2	Keeping things tidy
0 1 2	Doing arithmetic or accounts
0 1 2	Getting to work
0 1 2	Dressing and undressing
0 1 2	Bed making
0 1 2	Doing own work
0 1 2	Cleaning shoes
0 1 2	Touching door handles
0 1 2	Using toilet to urinate

0 1 2   Using toilet to defecate

0 1 2   Touching own genitals, petting,
            or sexual intercourse

0 1 2   Throwing things away

0 1 2   Visiting a hospital

0 1 2   Washing clothing

0 1 2   Handling waste or waste bins

0 1 2   Touching people or being touched

RESULTS

Total Scores: ■ 10 increase the possibility of obsessive-compulsive disorder (OCD), and further evaluation is recommended. Total scores ■ 20 are highly suggestive of OCD.

ALCOHOLISM

Screening for Problem Drinking

A.A. Grapevine, Inc. A.A. World Services, Inc.

1. Have you ever decided to stop drinking for a week or so, but only lasted for a couple of days? ❏ Yes ❏ No

2. Do you wish people would mind their own business about your drinking— stop telling you what to do? ❏ Yes ❏ No

3. Have you ever switched from one kind of drink to another in the hope that this would keep you from getting drunk? ❏ Yes ❏ No

4. Have you had to have an eye-opener upon awakening during the past year? ❏ Yes ❏ No

5. Do you envy people who can drink without getting into trouble? ❏ Yes ❏ No

6. Have you had problems connected with drinking during the past year? ❏ Yes ❏ No

7. Has your drinking caused trouble at home? ❏ Yes ❏ No

8. Do you ever try to get "extra"
    drinks at a party because you
    do not get enough?   ❏ Yes   ❏ No

9. Do you tell yourself you can stop
    drinking any time you want to, even
    though you keep getting drunk
    when you don't mean to?   ❏ Yes   ❏ No

10. Have you missed days of work or
    school because of drinking?   ❏ Yes   ❏ No

11. Do you have "blackouts"?   ❏ Yes   ❏ No
    (a "blackout" is when we have been drinking
    hours or days which we cannot remember.)

12. Have you ever felt that your life would
    be better if you did not drink?   ❏ Yes   ❏ No

RESULTS

If you answered **YES** to four or more questions, you are probably
in trouble with alcohol.

AL-ANON CODEPENDENCY QUESTIONS

From the Al-Anon Family Group Headquarters 20 Questions

1.   Do you constantly seek approval and affirmation?

2.   Do you fail to recognize your accomplishments?

3.   Do you fear criticism?

4.   Do you overextend yourself?

5.   Have you had problems with your own compulsive behavior?

6.   Do you have a need for perfection?

7.   Are you uneasy when your life is going smoothly, continually anticipating problems?

8.   Do you feel more alive in the midst of a crisis?

9.   Do you still feel responsible for others, as you did for the problem drinker in your life?

10.   Do you care for others easily, yet find it difficult to take care of yourself?

11.   Do you isolate yourself from other people?

12.   Do you respond with fear to authority figures and angry people?

13.   Do you feel that individuals and society in general are taking advantage of you?

14.   Do you have trouble with intimate relationships?

15. Do you confuse pity with love, as you did with the problem drinker?

16. Do you attract and/or seek people who tend to be compulsive and/or abusive?

17. Do you cling to relationships because you are afraid of being alone?

18. Do you often mistrust your own feelings, and he feelings expressed by others?

19. Do you find it difficult to identify and express your emotions?

20. Do you think parental drinking may have affected you?

NOTE: If there are mental illnesses or addictive behaviors in your family, you can ask yourself the same questions using those instead of problem drinking or other substance abuse or addiction.

DEPRESSION

The Hands Depression Screening Questionnaire

Copyright, President and Fellows of Harvard College and the National Mental Illness Screening Project, 1998

Fill in the response for each item based upon how you have been feeling for the past 2 weeks or longer. Scores do not confirm a diagnosis of depression. They do give an indication of what depression symptoms are like. It is recommended that you be evaluated by a licensed mental health professional for a more thorough and accurate assessment for a diagnosis.

Over the past two weeks,
how often have you: NONE SOME MOST ALL

1. been feeling low in energy, slowed down? ❑ ❑ ❑ ❑

2. been blaming yourself for things? ❑ ❑ ❑ ❑

3. had poor appetite? ❑ ❑ ❑ ❑

4. had difficulty falling asleep, staying asleep? ❑ ❑ ❑ ❑

5. been feeling hopeless about the future? ❑ ❑ ❑ ❑

6. been feeling sick? ❑ ❑ ❑ ❑

	NONE	SOME	MOST	ALL
7. been feeling no interest in things?	❑	❑	❑	❑
8. had feelings of worthlessness?	❑	❑	❑	❑
9. thought about or wanted to commit suicide?	❑	❑	❑	❑
10. had difficulty concentrating or making decisions?	❑	❑	❑	❑

RESULTS

Score horizontally each question by determining the numerical value for each answer given using the following values:

NONE or little of the time = 0   _____

SOME of the time = 1   _____

MOST of the time = 2   _____

ALL of the time = 3   _____

Score vertically all of the total values to
obtain your total score: _____

Score 0-8: Symptoms are not consistent with a major depressive episode. Presence of a major depressive episode is unlikely. A complete evaluation is not recommended except in the case of a positive response to the suicide question (item 9).

Score 9-16: Symptoms are consistent with a major depressive episode. Presence of a major depressive episode is likely. A complete evaluation is recommended. Severity level is typically mild or moderate, depending upon the degree of impairment.

Score 17-20: Symptoms are strongly consistent with criteria for a major depressive episode. Presence of major depressive episode is very likely. A complete evaluation is strongly recommended. In this higher range, the severity level may be more severe and require immediate attention.

EATING DISORDERS

The Eating Disorders Self Tests

Copyright © 1996. Mass Market Paperback. The Thin Disguise. Pam Vredevelt, Dr. Deborah Newman, Dr. Harry Beverly, Dr. Frank Minirth

Place a check next to each statement that is true for you.

❏   I have fasted to lose weight.

❏   I feel guilty when I eat.

❏   To control my weight, I purge and/or take
        laxatives/diuretics.

❏   I am never satisfied with myself.

❏   The number on the scales determines whether
        a day will be good or bad.

❏   I feel fat even though people say I'm thin.

❏   I have stolen food, diet pills, or laxatives.

❏   I am obsessive about food, i.e.; recipes,
        cookbooks, calories, etc.

❏   I binge on a regular basis.

❏   I'm afraid of losing control when I eat.

❑   I have the "all or nothing" feeling.

❑   I have rituals when I eat.

❑   I feel guilty and fear gaining weight if I miss exercising or eat as much as one bite more than I planned.

❑   I lie about what I eat.

❑   I hide my food.

❑   My menstrual periods have ceased or are irregular.

RESULTS

A **YES** to any of the questions may indicate the start of a problem. The more you have yes answers to, the more serious your problem may be. Please consult with a physician or mental health counselor familiar with Eating Disorders. Continue with the *Perfectionism Scale*.

PERFECTIONISM SCALE

Fill in the blank with the number that best describes how you think most of the time.

1 = Never 2 = Rarely 3 = Sometimes 4 = Often

1. If I don't set the highest standards for myself, I am likely to end up a second-rate person.   _____

2. People will probably think less of me if I make a mistake.   _____

3. If I cannot do something really well, there is little point in doing it at all.   _____

4. I should be upset if I make a mistake.   _____

5. If I try hard enough, I should be able to excel at anything I attempt.   _____

6. It is shameful for me to display weaknesses or foolish behavior.   _____

7. I shouldn't have to repeat the same mistakes many times.   _____

8. An average performance is bound to be unsatisfying to me.   _____

9. Failing at something important means I'm less of a person.   _____

10. If I scold myself for failing to live up to expectations, it will help me to do better in the future.   _____

RESULTS

Add up the scores. The total may generally be interpreted as follows:

10-20   Non-perfectionistic
21-30   Average tendencies toward perfectionism
31-40   Very perfectionistic

If you scored in the high range, you may wish to consult with a licensed mental health professional for further evaluation.

ATTENTION DEFICIT DISORDER

Attention Deficit Disorder Test

Copyright, Michael Kunz, M.D. and Waguih William IsHak, M.D.
New York University Department of Psychiatry, 1996.

Answer the following questions Yes if they have been present since childhood.

1.   Do you often have problems finishing tasks,
     or following through with projects?   _____

2.   Is it hard for you to get organized?   _____

3.   Is it hard for you to pay attention? Do you
     get easily distracted?   _____

4.   Do you tend to "tune out" and daydream a lot?   _____

5.   Do you have trouble starting tasks or
     projects? Do you put things off?   _____

6.   Do you often make impulsive decisions?
     Do you often abruptly change your plans
     without thinking through the consequences?   _____

7.   Do you often impulsively say things that
     make you unpopular, or that you later
     regret saying?   _____

8.   Do you suffer from frequent mood swings?   _____

9. Do you often engage in thrill-seeking activities including the potentially dangerous ones? _____

10. Are you often impatient, irritable? Do you feel restless, edgy? _____

11. Do you easily get frustrated? _____

12. Do you talk a lot and often interrupt others? _____

RESULTS

The more you have answered **YES** to any of these questions, the more serious your problem may be. Please consult with a physician or licensed mental health professional experienced in diagnosing and treating ADD.

PERSONALITY DISORDERS

Screening for Personality Disorders

Copyright, Benjamin J. Sadock, M.D. and Waguih William IsHak, M.D. New York University Department of Psychiatry, 1996.

Answer Yes to the following questions ONLY if they have been present over a long period of time causing distress or impairment in functioning.

1. Do you suspect that others are exploiting, harming or deceiving you? _____

2. Do you persistently bear grudges and not forget insults or injuries? _____

3. Do you almost always choose solitary activities? _____

4. Do you feel indifferent to praise or criticism of others? _____

5. Do you experience recurrent strange day dreams or fantasies? _____

6. Do you experience magical thinking that influences your behavior? _____

7. Do you repeatedly get into conflicts with the law? _____

8. Before age 18, have you been cruel to
    people or animals?   _____

9. Do you have a pattern of unstable and
    intense relationships with others?   _____

10. Do you have continuous feelings of emptiness? _____

11. Do you feel uncomfortable in situations
    where you are not the center of attention?   _____

12. Are you easily influenced by others or
    are you suggestible?   _____

13. Are you generally envious of other people?   _____

14. Are you preoccupied with unlimited
    success or ideal love?   _____

15. Are you unwilling to get involved
    with people unless you are certain
    of being liked?   _____

16. Do you view yourself as socially inept,
    personally unappealing or inferior to others? _____

17. Do you have a difficulty making everyday
    decisions without an excessive amount of
    advice and reassurance from others?   _____

18.   Are you preoccupied with fears of being
       left to take care of yourself?   _____

19.   Are you preoccupied with details, rules,
       lists, order, organization, or schedules?   _____

20.   Are you such a perfectionist that it interferes
       with your work?   _____

RESULTS

The more you have answered **YES** to any of these questions,
the more serious your problem may be. Please consult with a
physician or licensed mental health professional experienced in
diagnosing and treating personality disorders.

SEX ADDICTION

Questions based on 10 signs Dr. Patrick Carnes identified as indicating sexual addiction in his book *Don't Call It Love: Recovery from Sexual Addiction.*

1. Is your sexual behavior often out of your control?

2. Have there been severe consequences due to your sexual behavior?

3. Is there an inability to stop this high-risk behavior despite severe consequences?

4. Do you keep on trying, or wanting to try, to stop or limit your sexual behavior?

5. Do you use sex, sexual fantasy, porn in books, movies, on the Internet, as your primary way to relieve anxiety, to cope with emotions?

6. Has your sexual activity increased because past levels were no longer enough to relieve anxiety?

7. When you don't get enough sex, do you experience bad feelings that range from boredom to loneliness and isolation to depression?

8. Do you spend most of your time getting sex, having sex, thinking about sex you have had or are going to have, or recovering from previous sexual experiences?

9.   Do you neglect school, work, friendships, family life, other kinds of fun and activity because of sexual behavior?

10.   Is sex the driving force and interest in your life?

NOTE: You can substitute 'romance' or 'falling in love, being in love' for sex to discover if you are a romance addict.

STORY
JUST TELL ME YOU LOVE ME

"Missy was small for her age and looked, with her huge eyes and the fair hair that drifted round her face, much younger than sixteen.

It was the night of the Homecoming Dance, and her friends persuaded Missy to go with their group.

"No boy will dance with me—they treat me like someone's little sister."

"Who cares? We'll all dance together."

Missy cared. She cared desperately that not one boy, ever, had asked her out or even spoken to her as if she were a girl, not just somebody else's friend.

"It'll be cool," her friends insisted as they all crammed into one of the school buses sent around town to pick up a high school full of students for Homecoming.

"It'll be even more cool with some of this inside you," said someone, passing a bottle back over the bus seat to Missy.

There were lots of bottles being passed around the darkened bus, and there was a lot of laughter.

When their bus pulled up in front of the school gym, Missy as well as her friends was ready to have fun. Music roared through the open doors to greet them.

The gym was dark, with fairy lights strung above their heads, and a spinning mirrored ball. Colors flashed behind the school band on the stage. There were adult chaperones around the gym's edges, but they seemed to fade into the walls and out of Missy's consciousness.

With sudden bravery, Missy allowed herself to be pulled onto the dance floor. She danced as long as she could pretend anybody cared and then as always she retreated into the shadows.

"Hey," a male someone said softly near her ear. An arm circled her waist. Missy couldn't believe how lovely it felt, even if the boy had made a mistake and it wasn't Missy he wanted.

"Hey yourself," she leaned against him to whisper.

"Can't hear a thing in here. Want to go for a walk?"

Missy let herself be led out into the cooling evening. She shivered, and the male arm was quick to shield her from the night air.

"You look good tonight," said Charlie, his breath soft in Missy's hair, as he led her farther away from the school grounds and down the road where the town's small cemetery had forever provided privacy to young couples.

It provided Missy with privacy that night of the Homecoming Dance.

"Just tell me you love me, Charlie," was all she asked.

Charlie loved Missy that night and for a few more nights in the following weeks.

One evening, though, when Charlie couldn't make their date, he sent his best friend Troy to take Missy to the movie he had promised.

"I know someplace better than a movie," Troy said, "Do you mind?"

He had borrowed his father's car, and he drove Missy to a café downtown by the water where the harbor lights shone on the docks and the fishing boats rocked gently in the moonlight and the music from the juke box played softly in the darkness of the bar.

"They don't look too hard at IDs here," said Troy, as they slipped into a dim booth. "What'll you have?"

Missy was feeling really anxious. Had Charlie told Troy they'd had sex? Charlie wouldn't. He loved her. He had said so.

But after a few drinks, Missy began to relax. She wasn't sure Troy wasn't just as attentive, just as attractive, as Charlie. Maybe even more so.

Troy drove them to a motel blinking neon lights near a gas station at the edge of town.

It was the first of an endless series of motel rooms for Missy, and all she ever asked was,

"Just tell me you love me.**"**

SECTION THREE

MENTAL DISORDERS DICTIONARY

The definitions in this section are based on many of the books listed in the **Bibliography**, particularly:

- The American Psychiatric Association's *Diagnostic and Statistical Manual of Mental Disorders (4th ed.), DSM*

- The Annenberg Foundation's *Treating and Preventing Adolescent Mental Disorders*

- *50 Signs of Mental Illness,* Dr. James Whitney Hicks, Yale University Press

and published by **Bick Publishing House**:

- *Understand Your Self*
- *Addiction: The Brain Disease*
- *The Courage to Lead: Mental Illnesses & Addictions*
- *Living with Disabilities*
- *The Teen Brain Book: Who and What Are You?*
- *Are You Human, or What? Evolutionary Psychology*
- *Where's Your Head? Psychology for Teenagers*
- *Stop the Pain: Meditation for Teenagers*

The point of this **Mental Disorders Dictionary** is

- To provide further explanations of terms related to mental disorders and recovery.

- To supplement information in previous chapters.

- To stand on its own as a dictionary for the field of mental disorders and recovery.

abuse Repeated, excessive use of harmful substances, alcohol, drugs, nicotine, inhalants, or repeated, excessive repetition of harmful behaviors such as gambling, binge-eating, compulsive shopping, sexual acting-out.

Abusive use of substances and abusive behaviors not only often escalate into addictions, but can cause immediate harm: sexually transmitted diseases (STDs), AIDS; brain damage, insanity, death, arrest leading to jail time, car accidents, physical injury, manslaughter.

addiction Physical, emotional, mental craving for particular substances or behaviors, increasing tolerance that demands more and more to get high, the pain of withdrawal symptoms, and continued use despite adverse consequences.

alcoholism Progressive physical and mental disease that becomes worse over time. Symptoms include increasingly heavy drinking despite consequences: physical danger; legal jeopardy (arrests, car accidents); relationship, family, school, work problems; mood swings, personality changes, anxiety, headaches, nausea; difficulty in controlling amount, when to stop. In later stages, indications include increased tolerance, inability to cut down, blackout drinking, tremors, seizures, hallucinations, and other withdrawal symptoms. See 20 questions, p. 159. Causes: Research suggests about 50% genetic brain chemistry; 50% environment, stress, emotional and behavioral disorders, mental illness.

Alcoholics Anonymous World-wide support groups founded in 1935 by Bill Wilson, an alcoholic himself who discovered that the best help for an alcoholic was the support of other alcoholics who understood both the active addiction and how to stop drinking and stay stopped. He wrote *Alcoholics Anonymous* and *Twelve Steps and Twelve Traditions* of recovery from active alcoholism, and founded Alcoholics Anonymous, a worldwide network of groups for which there are no dues or fees, whose only requirement for membership is the desire to stop drinking. See offshoot support groups: **Al-Anon** (for families and friends of alcoholics); **Alateen** (for teen recovery, teens at risk); **Association for Children of Alcoholics; National Council on Alcoholism and Drug Dependence; National Institute on Alcohol Abuse and Alcoholism; Narcotics Anonymous** and more. See **Help and Resources, Organizations, Websites.**

anorexia nervosa Severe eating disorder: symptoms include an intense preoccupation with food and a fear of gaining weight. People with this disorder both limit food intake and binge-eat, then obsessed with over- eating, often purge with laxatives or by vomiting, take diet pills, push food around plate instead of eating. Body weight is low for height, they feel fat even when thin. Starvation to the point of death is possible without treatment. See 10 questions, p. 166. Causes: family and cultural beliefs about body size, brain chemistry, co-occurring psychiatric disorders, control issues. See bulimia, obsessive-compulsive disorder.

antisocial personality disorder Pattern of disregard for and violation of the rights of other people.

anxiety disorders Emotional disorders and illnesses often overwhelming, often progressive, often leading to substance addiction or addictive behaviors to obtain relief.

Generalized Anxiety Disorder (GAD): Excessive concerns over money, health, family, work. Physical symptoms may include trembling, headaches, irritability, sweating, nausea, difficulty in concentrating.

Panic Disorder: Repeated episodes of intense fear accompanied by physical symptoms such as chest pain, breathing difficulty, dizziness.

Agoraphobia: Fear for safety, of open spaces, fear of situations and places from which it is thought escape could be embarrassing or difficult. Physical symptoms are similar to panic attacks.

Social Phobia: Fear of being looked at in social situations, persistent performance anxiety, avoidance of people, places, activities that might expose the sufferer to shame. Physical symptoms include palpitations, sweating, trembling.

Also see: PTSD and OCD.

Studies show that teens with anxiety disorders are at greater risk for turning to smoking, drinking alcohol, using drugs, gambling, compulsive shopping, sex, overeating, and other compulsive-obsessive behaviors for relief.

attention deficit hyperactivity disorder (ADHD) Developmental disorder characterized by disorganized thinking, impulsiveness and problems in self-control, difficulty in completing tasks, forgetfulness, procrastination, inattention unless extremely passionate about a particular activity for which everything else may be sacrificed. Boys have the hyperactivity component more often than girls. Teens with these problems may be at risk for alcohol and drug abuse to ease their chronic anxiety.

autistic disorder Impaired development in social interaction and communication, impaired use of nonverbal behaviors such as lack of eye contact, lack of interest in friendships, self-stimulating repetitive behaviors and tics, self-absorption, no concept of the needs or points of view of others.

binging In terms of substance or behavior addictions, periodic rather than daily excessive, compulsive, unrestrained indulgence in substances like alcohol or drugs or in behaviors like eating, gambling, buying; may be symptomatic of full-blown disease of alcoholism or addiction; may be symptomatic of co-occurring mental disorders.

bipolar disorder Mood disorder (manic-depression) in which moods swing from manic (inflated self-esteem, hyperactive, unrestrained, hyperenergetic, impulsive activity, little need to sleep) to depressed (distinct drop in mood, often worst at waking and during late afternoon); daily loss of energy, either sleeping too much or cannot sleep; unplanned loss or increase of appetite; physical lethargy; disinterest even in favorite activities; difficulty in concentrating or even caring; moves in slow motion or may display agitation; feelings of deep sadness, even escalating to thoughts or plans of suicide; morbid self-centeredness, preoccupied with guilt, worthlessness.

blackouts Total memory loss for minutes, hours, even days, are one result of drug and alcohol abuse, a form of drug-induced brain damage in which the electrical storm caused by the drugs fouls up communication lines and memory storage in the brain.

body dysmorphic disorder BDD is an excessive concern with body image, imagined abnormalities or defects; this may result in overuse of dieting, plastic surgery, beauty supplies to correct perceived flaws in hair, skin, face, muscles, wrinkles, nose shape, breast size, buttocks, genitals; rituals involve constant self-preoccupation and examination; BBD is an unrealistic body perception no surgery or cosmetic ever addresses.

bulimia nervosa An eating disorder defined as periods of binge-eating in which large quantities of food are eaten, and then purged (vomiting, laxatives, diuretics) or through excessive exercise. Food is used addictively as a reward or to ward off anxiety, to comfort, to escape reality. Bulimics eat too fast and too much; they prefer to eat alone to hide quantity; guilt, self-hate, depression occur after binging.

club drugs Drugs such as Ecstasy. Rohypnol, Ketamine and other date-rape drugs can cause memory loss, brain damage, and death, according to the National Institute on Drug Abuse.

codependency In *Codependent No More*, Melody Beattie defines a codependent as "anyone who has let another person's behavior affect him or her, and who is obsessed with controlling that person's behavior." Person addiction includes a fear of being alone or abandoned, a need to be needed so intense that mates and friends are usually chosen among other dependent or addicted personalities. See Al-Anon's 10 questions, p. 161.

compulsion Repetitive behavior such as hand-washing, counting, aligning objects, repeating words silently in order to reduce anxiety or distress.

co-occurring disorders, mental illnesses, psychiatric problems
A brain hijacked by drugs usually has an increased possibility of previous and ongoing anxiety disorder, depression, PTSD, learning disabilities, schizophrenia, ADHD. Addiction treatment must include treating the mental disorder or relapse will likely occur.

cutting An addiction to self-inflicted physical pain sometimes for attention, usually to relieve intense psychological anguish: knife, scissors, razor, whatever is available is used on stomach (where it won't show), arms, legs, face where it will show.

Cybersex addiction (Internet, TV pornography) Release from anxiety, depression, loneliness, like any other drug or addictive behavior, with the added component of intimacy fears, possible social or environmental phobias.

date rape Forced sexual assault by a person known to the victim, most usually perpetrated on adolescent females, but even on adolescent males, by males.

denial Psychological mechanism, often unconscious, used by alcoholics / addicts, to minimize abuse and dependency in order to protect their habit; friends and families of alcoholics / addicts also use the mechanism to avoid facing and dealing with the problem.

dependence More severe condition than abuse; medical professionals will look for physical symptoms such as: 1) tolerance (when a person needs more of a drug to achieve the desired effect or to ward off withdrawal symptoms) and 2) withdrawal symptoms when drug use is reduced or stopped. Professionals also look for behavioral criteria such as 1) being unable to stop once using starts, 2) avoidance of responsibilities, work, school, social activities to spend more time using; 3) continued use despite personality, health, and relationship deterioration.

depression Major depression is a mood disorder the symptoms of which are a severe drop in mood, a loss of interest and pleasure in life: the profound sadness and loss of joy and energy are not situational but physiological, neurochemical, genetic in origin.
See also manic-depression or bipolar disorder.

detoxification The first stage, but not the only stage, of treatment for alcoholism and drug addiction, is to cleanse, deprive the system of the toxic substance: sometimes rest is enough, but after prolonged and heavy use of alcohol, opiates, tranquilizers, supervised medical treatment of withdrawal symptoms reduces the severity, pain, craving. After stabilization, life changes and continued treatment and rehabilitation are necessary, just as for any other progressive disease such as diabetes.

drugs Please see pages 192-195 for drugs and alcohol list and its schedule of effects, risks, and withdrawal symptoms is partial. Further numbers and addresses for help are listed in an appendix at the back of this book. Also, see *A Teen's Guide to Living Drug-Free* by Bettie B. Youngs and Jennifer Leigh Youngs.

dual diagnosis Presence of one or more psychiatric disorders as well as alcoholism or drug addiction, such as depression, anxiety disorder, schizophrenia, bipolar disorder, OCD, or one of the other behavioral addictions.

eating disorders See anorexia, bulimia.

flashbacks Imaginary recurring of previous experiences due to PTSD, use of hallucinagens, stressors, or an unspecified psychotic disorder.

gambling Pathologically addicted, compulsive gamblers are preoccupied with the high of risk-taking, and obsess over past, present, and future gambling, even if it means financial ruin. This is often accompanied by systems and rituals based on the gambler's beliefs in the ability to control outcomes.

gender identity disorder Preoccupation with intense need to get rid of secondary sex characteristics based on identification with a different sex; the belief that he or she was born the wrong sex.

impulse control disorders and addictions See obsessive compulsive disorder (OCD), pathological gambling, compulsive shopping, body dysmorphic disorder (BDD), eating disorders, alcohol and

DRUGS AND ALCOHOL

	EFFECTS	RISKS	WITHDRAWAL
Depressants			
ALCOHOL Beer, Wine, Hard Liquor	distortion of reality impaired coordination exaggerated emotions impaired judgment slurred speech, aggression	blackouts sex drive loss brain damage death	insomnia anxiety seizures DT's (delirium tremens) fatality, strokes possible
BARBITURATES Nembutal, Phenobarbital	bloodshot eyes argumentativeness confusion, dizziness	brain damage coma, death	convulsions, nausea cramps, delirium fatality, strokes possible
TRANQUILIZERS Ativan, BZD, Klonopin, Librium, Valium, Xanax	confusion sleepiness detachment	heart problems overdose, death chronic anxiety	agitation, cramps, nausea, tremors fatality, strokes possible
Stimulants			
COCAINE Crack (smoked cocaine)	excessive activity and talk, agitation, belligerence, dilated pupils	brain seizures, 'bugs crawling on skin,' insomnia, violence, paranoia, head & stomach aches, depression	pain, cravings, delusions

AMPHETAMINES METHAMPHETAMINES Crank (Street name)	same and more	same plus tics, convulsions	delirium, suicidal thoughts
RITALIN	agitation, anxiety talkativeness	anxiety, insomnia, irritability	fatigue, headaches
CAFFEINE (Tea, Coffee, Energy Drinks)	increased heart rate, activity and talk	gastric pains, ulcers anxiety, insomnia, jittery nerves	headaches fatigue irritability
NICOTINE (cigarettes, cigars,) pipe tobacco, snuff	increased blood pressure and heart rate, reduced appetite	cancer, heart and lung disease, stroke, wheeze	aggression intense craving depression concentration problems
Opiates/Narcotics			
HEROIN MORPHINE OPIUM PRESCRIPTION PAINKILLERS*	apathy, constricted pupils slowed breathing, possible needle marks, impaired thinking, high risk of illness, stupor	collapsed veins, impotence, coma, overdose, death	pain nausea cramps chills intense cravings

Vicodin, oxycodone, OxyContin, Percocet, Percodan

DRUGS AND ALCOHOL

	EFFECTS	RISKS	WITHDRAWAL
Inhalants			
CONSUMER AEROSOLS, FREON PAINT, NAIL POLISH REMOVERS, AIRPLANE GLUE, CLEANING SOLVENTS	irrational behavior, runny nose, drowsiness, slurred speech, distortion of reality	brain damage coma, death asphyxiation hallucinations	confusion headache
DEPRESSIVE INHALANTS Amyl nitrate Butyl nitrate	above, plus flushed face, neck	blood vessel damage, heart attack	
Cannabinoids			
MARIJUANA	craving for sweets less inhibited red eyes forgetfulness	memory loss lethargy psychosis uncontrolled laughter	anxiety fatigue despair
HASHISH	same, plus distorted senses, inability to think clearly	same, plus impotence, loss of reasoning ability	same, plus anorexia insomnia

Hallucinogens, Club Or Designer Drugs: Psychedelics

LSD (ACID)	sensory distortion hallucinations, insomnia, mood swings, violence, time loss, dilated pupils	bad trips, catatonia, schizoid behavior, coma, convulsions, permanent loss of reality	flashbacks insomnia
MDMA (ECSTASY)	confusion, insomnia, distorted reality, accelerated heart rate, hallucinations	brain damage, convulsions, death	insomnia, irritability

Note: With LSD, MDMA, as well as marijuana, you don't know what extra dangerous chemicals or in what possibly fatal doses dealers have mixed with the drug.

KETAMINE	delusions, dissociation, babbling, bad taste	amnesia, delirium, death	anxiety, depression
ROHYPNOL (Date Rape Drug)	confusion, sleepiness	blackouts, confusion, date rape, death	agitation, tremors, cramps
PCP (Angel Dust)	delusions, self-destructive behavior, unnatural stare, violence	flashbacks, suicidal anxiety, confusion, isolation	cravings, depression, insomnia, tremors

drug addictions, kleptomania: also on the list of impulse control disorders are trichotillomania (pulling out hair compulsively from any part of the body); hypochondria (fear derived from imagining signs of medical illness despite being healthy); and Tourette's Disorder (uncontrollable sudden rapid movements, words, or sounds).

internet addiction disorder Cyberpsychologists, according to *U.S. News & World Report*, define IAD as a preoccupation with a virtual world that substitutes for the real world, interfering with real relationships, studies, work, friends and family. When deprived of their Internet time, those with IAD grow anxious or depressed as in withdrawal from any other addiction. Also destructive in Internet addiction is the availability of drugs, porn, internet sex, gambling, and the chat rooms also accessible to perverts preying on the innocent.

jealousy In relationships, jealousy refers to an unreasonable fear of losing an important relationship. Pathological jealousy is often a sign of a personality disorder.

kleptomania Repeated and compulsive stealing for excitement, psychological reward, or to relieve anxiety: this disorder is distinguished from shoplifting which is based on personal gain.

love Affection, passion with no dependency, no attachment, no need or neediness.

major depression Loss of interest and pleasure in life, a deep sadness and fatigue, based not in external situations but in one's own brain chemistry.

manic depression Mood swings from manic (inflated self-esteem, grandiosity, hyperactive, unrestrained behavior, little need to sleep, impulsive activity like falling in or out of love, compulsive shopping sprees, sudden traveling) to depressive (see major depression symptoms). Unpredictable, frightening mood disorder of the brain chemistry, not based on external situations.

mood State of emotional being such as sadness, happiness, fear (boredom and anxiety are low-grade states of fear).

mood disorders See Depression, Bipolar Disorder, Anxiety Disorder.

narcotics Opioid-based drugs, legal and illegal, prescription, club, and street. The United States DEA (Drug Enforcement Administrations) has imposed the Controlled Substances Act with schedules (lists) of those drugs used for medical purposes such as OxyContin and those drugs for which there is no current medical use such as heroin.

Narcotics Anonymous A program for those addicted to drugs based on the 12 Step Program of Alcoholics Anonymous. See help numbers list at the back of this book.

obsessive-compulsive disorder (OCD) A form of anxiety disorder; people with OCD suffer from recurrent, persistent, unwanted, unrealistic thoughts and obsessions; ritualistic, unnecessary, and obsessive behaviors like counting and placing objects in a certain order; constant washing of hands, checking and rechecking lights, locks, the stove. The thoughts are the obsessions; the behaviors are the compulsions to overcome irrational, obsessive fears. For help, see Help and Resources lists: Anxiety Disorders Association of America, National Institute of Mental Health (NIMH).

overeating Eating more than is appropriate for height and body frame, resulting in obesity; this may be the result of food addiction, anxiety disorder, eating disorder, glandular imbalance, gene pool factors, developmental delays, the constant availability of inexpensive, supersized junk food, our sedentary lives.

over-the-counter medications Health drugs that do not require a prescription such as cold medications, cough syrups, pain killers, laxatives—all can be used and abused and turned into addictions.

people addiction See popularity addiction.

personality disorders Faulty perception of oneself and one's relationship with others, leading to unfulfilled expectations: inflexible inability to perceive disordered self makes it difficult to change. Several personality disorders may coexist: **borderline personality disorder** symptoms, based on fear of abandonment, include unstable fluctuations between neediness and hypercritical rejection, inflation of self and excessive criticism; **obsessive-compulsive personality disorder** symptoms are a preoccupation with perfectionism (living up to conditioned standards), workaholism, and the need to control others.

popularity addiction What originated as an evolutionary imperative for a pack animal like humans—survival depends on acceptance by the group for food and protection—is exaggerated into an obsessive, dependent need for everyone's good opinion and constant approval.

possessions addiction An addiction to one's stuff, and to the acquisition of more stuff as a form of security; sometimes accompanied by an inability to throw anything away, sometimes referred to as pack-ratting or hoarding.

post-traumatic stress disorder (PTSD) Severe anxiety reaction to the shock of past painful events such as physical abuse, drug experiences, violence in families, on the streets, in war: PTSD often results in drug abuse to alleviate the psychological pain. Flashbacks.

panic An attack of intense anxiety, accompanied by the physical symptoms of sweat or chills, trembling, pulse and heartbeat racing, difficulty breathing, butterflies or stomach cramp, feelings of terror, even that you are going to die of heart attack or stroke.

paranoia Unwarranted feeling others are trying to harm you, even kill you.

psychosis To be psychotic is to be out of touch with reality.

recovery Ending the use of addictive chemical substances and addictive behaviors involving the rewiring of brain circuits altered by drugs, alcohol, and maladaptive behaviors through treatment: whether therapy, 12-step programs, medication or any combination of these.

romance addiction The high is the neurophysiological chemistry of being in love, the mental and emotional attraction that includes the excitement of meeting of emotional, sexual, and mental needs, rescue needs, mutual dependencies, the need for exclusivity and the immature need for possession of another human being. Fear of loss heightens the above mixture of excitement, as does fear of discovery. May co-occur with, but is not identical to, sex addiction, the need for the high of constant sexual stimulation, sometimes with the same partner, often with the need for a constant change of sexual partners, even of strangers.

scheduled drugs The Drug Enforcement Administration (DEA) lists legal and illegal drugs according to their potential for addiction; a partial list includes:

Schedule I drugs are illegal, with the most potential for addiction: heroin, crack cocaine, Ecstasy.

Schedule II drugs, also with potential for addiction, are considered to have medical use, such as morphine, oxycodone, cocaine.

Schedule III drugs include some barbiturates, steroids, ketamine.

Schedule IV drugs include antianxiety drugs and sedatives like Xanax, Librium, Clonopin.

Schedule V drugs are over-the-counter preparations like cough and cold medicines.

schizophrenia Psychotic disturbance that may include a loss of contact with reality, the experience of delusions and hallucinations, inner-directed behaviors that may seem purposeless and unconnected to the outside environment, including repetitive, obsessive-compulsive, ritualistic behaviors.

self addiction Rigid clinging to one's own ideas, opinions, habits, one's own importance.

self-injury, self-mutilation Injuring oneself by making cuts or scratches on one's own body with an object sharp enough to break the skin and make it bleed, or burn the skin with the end of a lighted cigarette or match, evidenced by scars or marks on the body, often on the belly or legs and thus hidden by clothing: a desperate way of coping with terrible emotions or a bad situation, feelings too difficult to bear such as rage, sorrow, rejection, terror, emptiness, through the distraction of immediate physical pain: cutting often co-occurs with depression, obsessive thinking, other compulsive behaviors.

sex addiction Progressive disease like alcoholism and drug dependency in which the addict requires more and more of the high released by chemical/sexual hormones to satisfy the body's cravings: healthy relationships to other people, work, school, everything is sacrificed to temporary sexual pleasure, and this is accompanied by guilt, shame, fear of discovery of their out-of-control behavior, whether this occurs with people, or online with cybersex or pornography: compulsion to obsess about or to engage in frequent sexual activity regardless of health, legality, or other obligations and relationships: compulsive sex addicts are often unable to achieve emotional intimacy. See Sex Addicts Anonymous.

shoplifting When stealing for personal gain, the paying of debts, to support the self and solve money issues instead of working for a living. The issues are different from the addictive behavior used for a thrill, a high, a 'rush.' See Kleptomania. See CASA (Cleptomania and Shoplifters Anonymous).

stress Temporary mental health problem, see anxiety.

suicide The taking of one's own life, the third leading cause of death among teenagers and young adults.

substance abuse Repeated use of alcohol or other drugs, less severe than addiction in that the tolerance that requires increasingly greater quantities has not yet developed, but that still interferes with school, work, relationships, obligations.

tolerance A major symptom of addiction, in that increased amounts of alcohol and drugs are required to achieve the same high over time.

trauma Psychological scars, as distressing as physical scars, left by terrifying events, such as anxiety, depression, dissociation, PTSD symptoms resulting from horrors such as physical trauma, abuse, rape, physical assault, combat, natural disasters, death of someone close.

treatment Aided, supported recovery from illness, physical or mental.

withdrawal The physical and emotional/psychological symptoms, always uncomfortable, sometimes painful, experienced by an addict deprived of the substance, activity, person, place, or thing to which or on which a dependency has been formed.

SECTION FOUR

HOTLINES, HELP AND RESOURCES, ORGANIZATIONS, WEBSITES

HOTLINES

National Hopeline Network
201 North 23rd Street
Purcellville, PA 20132
Tel: 800-SUICIDE (784-2433)
www.hopeline.com
Hopeline can connect you to a suicide crisis center in your area.

National Sex Assault Hotline
Rape, Abuse, and Incest
National Network (RAINN)
Tel: 800-656-HOPE (4673)
www.rainn.org

Health Hotlines
www.sis.nlm.gov/hotlines
A listing of dozens of hotlines pertaining to medical and mental illnesses.

Government Agencies

**National Institute of
Mental Health (NIMH)**
6001 Executive Blvd
Bethesda, MD 20892
Tel: 866-615-6464
www.nimh.nih.gov

**National Mental Health
Association (NMHA)**
2001 North Beauregard Street
Alexandria, VA 22311
Tel: 703-684-7722,
800-969-6642
www.nmha.org

Organizations

Al-Anon
1600 Corporate Landing Pkwy.
Virginia Beach, VA 23454
(757) 563-1600
www.al-anon.org

Alcoholics Anonymous World Services, Inc.
P.O. Box 459
Grand Central Station
New York, NY 10163
(212)870-3400
www.alcoholicsanonymous.
org

American Academy of Child and Adolescent Psychiatry
3615 Wisconsin Ave., NW
Washington, DC 20016
(202)966-7300
www.aacap.org

American Anorexia/Bulimia Association, Inc.
165 West 46 St. Suite 1108
New York, NY 10036
(212)575-6200
www.aabainc.org

American Foundation for Suicide Prevention
120 Wall St. 22nd Fl.
New York, NY 10005
(800)333-AFSP
www.afsp.org

American Psychiatric Association
1000 Wilson Blvd.
Arlington, VA 22209
703-907-730o
www.psych.org

American Psychological Association
750 First Street NE
Washington, DC 20002
202-336-5500
www.apa.org

American Self-Help Clearinghouse
Northwest Covenant Medical Center
25 Pocono Road
Denville, NJ 07834
(973)625-3037
www.cmhc.com / selfhelp

Anxiety Disorders Association of America
11900 Parklawn Dr. Suite 100
Rockville, MD 20852
(301)231-9350
www.adaa.org

Children and Adults with Attention Deficit and Hyperactivity Disorders
8181 Professional Place #201
Landover, MD 20785
(800)233-4050
www.chadd.org

National Clearinghouse for Alcohol and Drug Information
P.O. Box 2345
Rockville, MD 20847
(800)729-6686
www.health.org

American Association on Mental Retardation
444 North Capitol Street NW
Washington, DC 20001
899-424-3688
www.aamr.org

Autism Society of America
7910 Woodmont Avenue
Bethesda, MD 20814
800-3288476
www.autism-society.org

Depression and Bipolar Support Alliance
730 N. Franklin St. Suite 501
Chicago, IL 60610
(800) 826-3632
www.dbsalliance.org

National Mental Health Association
1021 Prince St.
Alexandria, VA 22314
(800)969-NMHA
www.nmha.org

Obsessive Compulsive Anonymous World Services
P.O. Box 215
New Hyde Park, NY 11040
(516)741-4901
www.ocfoundation.org

Obsessive Compulsive Foundation
676 State Street
New Haven, CT 06511
(203) 401-2070
www.ocfoundation.org

National Schizophrenia Foundation
403 Seymour Avenue
Lansing, MI 48933
800-482-9534
www.nsfoundation.org

BIBLIOGRAPHY
& YOUNG ADULT
READING LIST

M ajor sources for facts and statistics in this book, aside from the following texts, were newspapers, journals, magazines, especially *U. S. News & World Report, Scientific American, National Geographic,* government publications, almanacs, public television specials, documentaries, news broadcasts.

Many of the books listed have already been mentioned in the text of this book.

Teen Series Published by Bick Publishing House

Carlson, Dale and Hannah Carlson, M.Ed., C.R.C. *Where's Your Head? Psychology for Teenagers.* 3rd edition. Branford, CT: Bick Publishing House, 2013. A general introduction for adults and young adults to the structure of personality formation, the meaning of intelligence, the mind, feelings, behaviors, biological and cultural agenda, and how to transform our conditioning and ourselves.

Carlson, Dale. *Are You Human, or What?* Madison, CT: Bick Publishing House, 2008. Teen guide to the new science of evolutionary psychology, what instincts and behaviors we have inherited from our animal past, what continues to be useful for survival, what we must change in order to survive at all and graduate from human to humane.

_____. *Addiction: The Brain Disease*. Branford, CT: Bick Pubishing House, 2012. Young adult guide to the physical, emotional, social, psychological disease of addiction.

_____. *Stop the Pain: Teen Meditations*. Madison, CT: Bick Publishing House, 1999. Self knowledge is true meditation: ways to lose the anxiety, hurt, conflict, pain, depression, addictions, loneliness, and to move on.

_____. *Understand Your Self*. Branford, CT: Bick Pubishing House, 2013. Young adult guide to understanding one's self, others, relationships to people, society, school, work, the world.

_____. Edited by Nancy Teasdale, B.S. Physics, *The Teen Brain Book: Who and What Are You?* Madison, CT: Bick Publishing House, 2005. Teen guide to understanding the brain, how it works, how you got the way you are, how to rewire yourself, your personality, and what makes you suffer.

_____. Foreword by Dialogue Director Kishore Khairnar. *Talk: Teen Art of Communication*, Madison, CT: Bick Publishing House, 2006. Close, powerful relationships are based on communication. How to talk to yourself, to others, to parents, teachers, bosses, sisters, brothers, friends, boyfriends and girlfriends, to groups, to people you don't like, to God.

Carlson, Hannah, M.Ed.,C.R.C. *Living with Disabilities. 2nd edition.* Madison, CT: Bick Publishing House, 1997. A 6-volume compendium with sections that describe symptoms, origins, treatments for mental disorders, learning, disabilities, brain defects and injuries. Includes: *I Have a Friend with Mental Illness*.

_____. *The Courage to Lead: Start Your Own Support Group, Mental Illnesses and Addictions.* Madison, CT: Bick Publishing House, 2001.

Krishnamurti, J. *What Are You Doing with Your Life? Books on Living for Teens.* Ojai, California: Krishnamurti Foundation of America, 2001.

_____. *Relationships; To Oneself, to Others, to the World, Books on Living for Teens.* Ojai, California: Krishnamurti Foundation of America, 2008. Your own understanding of how your human brain and mind work, the difference between intellect and intelligence, is the self-knowledge necessary to guide your life, not the past or other people's opinions. You are your own responsibility, not someone else's.

OTHER SOURCES

Alcoholics Anonymous. Alcoholics Anonymous (The Big Book). New York: Alcoholics Anonymous Wold Services, Inc. 2001.

Al-Anon's Twelve Steps/Twelve Traditions. New York: Alcoholics Anonymous World Services, Inc. 2001.

Beattie, Melody. *Codependent No More.* Center City, MN: Hazelden, 1992.

Cobain, Bev. *When Nothing Matters Anymore: A survival Guide for Depressed Teens.* Minneapolis, MN: Free Spirit Publishing, 1998.

American Psychiatric Association: *Diagnostic and Statistical Manual of Mental Disorders (4thEd.)* Washington, 1994, American Psychiatric Association.

American Self-Help Clearinghouse. *The Self-Help Sourcebook. Your Guide to Community and Online Support Groups. Sixth Ed.* New Jersey, American Self-Help Clearinghouse, 1998.

C. Roy. *Obsessive-Compulsive Disorder. A Survival Guide for Family and Friends.* New York: Obsessive-Compulsive Anonymous, 1993.

Covey, Sean. *The 7 Habits of Highly Effective Teens.* New York: Simon & Schuster, 1998.

Granet, Roger, MD., Levinson, Robin Karol. *If You Think You Have Depression (The Dell Guides For Mental Health).* New York: Mass Market Paperback, 1998.

Granet, Roger, MD., Ferber, Elizabeth. *Why Am I Up, Why Am I Down?: Understanding Bi-polar Disorder (The Dell Guides For Mental Health).* New York: Mass Market Paperback, 1999.

Gwinnell, Esther, MD, Christine Adamec. *The Encyclopedia of Addictions and Addictive Behaviors.* New York: Facts on File, Inc., 2006.

Hallowell, Edward, M. M.D. Ratey, John J., M.D. *Driven To Distraction: Recognizing and Coping with Attention Deficit Disorder from Childhood Through Adulthood.* New York: Pantheon Books, 1994.

Hoffman, John, and Froemke, Susan, Editors. *Addiction: Why Can't They Just Stop?* New York: Rodale, Inc. and HBO, 2007.

Kaysen, Susanna. *Girl Interrupted.* New York: Vintage Books, 1994.

March, John, S. M.D. *Anxiety Disorder in Children and Adolescents.* New York: Guilford Press, 1995.

Ketchan, Katherine, and Nicholas A. Pace, M.D. *Teens Under the Influence*. New York: Ballentine Books, 2003.

Youngs, Bettie B., Ph.D., Ed.D. and Youngs, Jennifer Leigh. *A Teen's Guide to Living Drug-Free*. Deerfield Beach, FL: Health Communications, Inc. 2003.

INDEX

BICK PUBLISHING HOUSE
PRESENTS
NEW! Books for Young Adults
by ALA Notable Book Author

OUT OF ORDER
Young Adult Manual of
Mental Illness and Recovery
by Dale Carlson and Dr. Michael Bower
Pictures by Carol Nicklaus

MENTAL ILLNESSES • PERSONALITY DISORDERS
LEARNING PROBLEMS • INTELLECTUAL DISABILITIES
TREATMENT AND RECOVERY

- What is mental illness? What are the symptoms? Do you need help?
- How to find the right kind of help; how to take responsibility yourself
- Psychoses: Mood Disorders, Anxiety and Personality Disorders, Addictions, Sex and Gender Disorders, Learning and Intellectual Disabilities
- Recovery: Treatments, Therapies, Medications, Support Groups
- Self-tests: Mental Health Disorders Dictionary, Resources, Websites, Organizations

ALL HUMANS SUFFER MENTALLY. HELP IS OUT THERE.

DALE CARLSON: Author of dozens of books for young adults, with 3 ALA Notable Book Awards, the Christopher Award, YALSA Best Picks, VOYA Honor Book, 3 New York Public Library Best Books for Teens, 2 Independent Press Medals, 4 *ForeWord* Best Books of the Year

Publishers Weekly: "A practical focus on psychological survival."

School Library Journal: "Fan of Dale Carlson's books for years."

New York Times Book Review: "She writes with intelligence and wit."

Available in print and ebook.
Illustrations, Index, Resources, Websites
256 pages, $14.95, ISBN: 978-1-884158-37-7

BICK PUBLISHING HOUSE
PRESENTS
Books for Young Adults

UNDERSTAND YOUR SELF
by Dale Carlson and Kishore Khairnar, Physicist
Pictures by Carol Nicklaus

A practical manual for the. Understanding of oneself. Self-Knowledge Is the Basis for Relationship and the End of Human Loneliness

"I've been a fan of Dale Carlson's books for years. *Understand Your Self* leaves no doubt that this author knows how to write for teens about what is going on in their lives and brains."
— *Dodie Ownes, School Library Journal*

Available in print and ebook.
Illustrations, Index, Resources, Websites
192 pages, $14.95, ISBN: 978-1-884158-36-0

ADDICTION: THE BRAIN DISEASE
by Dale Carlson and Hannah Carlson, M.Ed., LPC
Pictures by Carol Nicklaus

Young adult guide to the physical, emotional, social, psychological disease of addiction.

"This book unlocks the door of hope to any suffering from the disease of addiction to substances and/or behaviors. "
— *Jason DeFrancesco, Yale-New Haven Medic*

Available in print and ebook.
Illustrations, Index, Resources, Self-Screening Tests, Help Telephone Numbers, Websites
114 pages, $14.95, ISBN978-1-884158-35-3

THE TEEN BRAIN BOOK *Who & What Are You?*
by Dale Carlson. Pictures by Carol Nicklaus.
Edited by Nancy Teasdale, B.S. Physics

Understand your own brain, how it works, how you got the way you are, how to rewire yourself, your personality, what makes you suffer

"Quality read for young adults." — *Midwest Book Review*

ForeWord Bronze Book of the Year
Illustrations, Index, 256 pages, $14.95.
ISBN: 1-884158-29-3

BICK PUBLISHING HOUSE
PRESENTS
Books for Young Adults

TALK: Teen Art of Communication
By Dale Carlson
Foreword by Kishore Khairnar, Dialogue Director

Close, powerful relationships are based on communication:
Humans are wired for talk...communication must be learned.
Teen guide to dialogue and communication.

"Essential reading."— Jim Cox, *Midwest Book Review*

ForeWord Book of the Year
*I*llustrations, 192 pages, $14.95, ISBN: 1-884158-32-3

IN AND OUT OF YOUR MIND
Teen Science: Human Bites
By Dale Carlson. Edited by Kishore Khairnar, M.S. Physics

Teens learn about our minds, our bodies, our Earth, the
Universe, the new science—in order to make their own
decisions. This book makes science fun and attainable.

"Heady stuff." — School Library Journal

New York Public Library Best Book for Teens
International Book of the Month
Illustrations, Index, 256 Pages, $14.95
ISBN: 1-884158-27-7

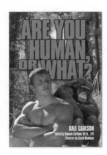

ARE YOU HUMAN, OR WHAT?
Evolutionary Psychology for Teens

We have evolved from reptile to mammal to human. Can we
mutate, evolve into humane?

"Are You Human, or What? reminds us that we—as nervous,
curious people—are not alone. Everyone suffers—and everyone can do something about it."
— Meghan Ownbey, Teen Editor

ForeWord Book of the Year
Illustrations, 224 pages, $14.95, ISBN: 978-1-884158-33-9

BICK PUBLISHING HOUSE
PRESENTS
Books for Young Adults

STOP THE PAIN: Teen Meditations
Teens have their own ability for physical and mental meditation to end psychological pain.

- What Is meditation: many ways
- When, where, with whom to meditate
- National directory of resources, centers

"Much good advice...." — *School Library Journal*

New York Public Library Best Book for Teens
Independent Publishers Award
Illustrations, Index, 224 pages, $14.95; ISBN: 1-884158-23-4

WHERE'S YOUR HEAD? Psychology for Teenagers

- Behaviors, feelings, personality formation
- Parents, peers, drugs, sex, violence, discrimination, addictions, depression
- Joys of relationship, friends, skills
- Insight, meditation, therapy

"A practical focus on psychological survival skills."
— *Publishers Weekly*

New York Public Library Books
YA Christopher Award Book
Illustrations, Index, 320 pages, $14.95;
ISBN: 1-884158-19-6

GIRLS ARE EQUAL TOO: The Teenage Girl's How-to-Survive Book
The female in our society: how to change.

- Girls growing up, in school, with boys
- Sex and relationships
- What to do about men, work, marriage, our culture: the fight for survival.

"Clearly documented approach to cultural sexism."
— *School Library Journal*

ALA Notable Book
Illustrations, Index, 256 pages, $14.95; ISBN: 1-884158-18-8

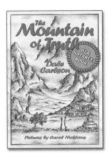

BICK PUBLISHING HOUSE
PRESENTS
Books on Living for Young Adults

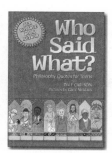

WHO SAID WHAT?
Philosophy Quotes for Teens
by Dale Carlson. Pictures by Carol Nicklaus

Teen guide to comparing philosophies of the great thinkers of the ages: form your own philosophy.

"Thought-provoking guide." —School Library Journal

VOYA Honor Book
YALSA Quickpicks for Teens
Illustrations, Index, 256 pages, $14.95.
ISBN: 1-884158-28-5

TEEN RELATIONSHIPS
To Oneself, To Others, To the World
By J. Krishnamurti. Edited by Dale Carlson

- What is relationship?
- To your friends, family, teachers
- In love, sex, marriage
- To work, money, government, society, nature
- Culture, country, the world, God, the universe

J. Krishnamurti spoke to young people all over the world. "When one is young." He said, "one must be revolutionary, not merely in revolt...to be psychologically revolutionary means non-acceptance of any pattern."

Illustrations, Index, 288 Pages, $14.95. ISBN: 1-888004-25-8

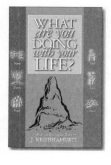

WHAT ARE YOU DOING WITH YOUR LIFE?
Books on Living for Teenagers
By J. Krishnamurti. Edited by Dale Carlson

Teens learn to understand the self, the purpose of life, work, education, relationships.

The Dalai Lama calls Krishnamurti "one of the greatest thinkers of the age." Time magazine named Krishnamurti, along with Mother Teresa, "one of the five saints of the 20th century."

Translated into five languages.
Illustrations, Index, 288 Pages, $14.95. ISBN: 1-888004-24-X

BICK PUBLISHING HOUSE
PRESENTS

Books for Health & Recovery

THE COURAGE TO LEAD—Start Your Own Support Group: Mental Illnesses & Addictions
By Hannah Carlson, M.Ed., C.R.C.

Diagnoses, Treatments, Causes of Mental Disorders, Screening tests, Life Stories, Bibliography, National and Local Resources.

"Invaluable supplement to therapy."
— *Midwest Book Review*

Illustrations, Index, 192 pages, $14.95;
ISBN: 1-884158-25-0

LIVING WITH DISABILITIES
By Hannah Carlson, M.Ed., CRC • Dale Carlson

Endorsed by Doctors, Rehabilitation Centers, Therapists, and Providers of Services for People with Disabilities

"Excellent, informative, accurate."
— Alan Ecker, M.D., Clinical Associate Professor at Yale

6-Volume Compendium
ISBN: 1-884158-15-3, $59.70

STOP THE PAIN: Adult Meditations
By Dale Carlson

Discover meditation: you are your own best teacher. How to use meditation to end psychological suffering, depression, anger, past and present hurts, anxiety, loneliness, the daily problems with sex and marriage, relationships, work and money.

"Carlson has drawn together the diverse elements of the mind, the psyche, and the spirit of science...Carlson demystifies meditation using the mirrors of insight and science to reflect what is illusive and beyond words." — R.E. Mark Lee, Director, Krishnamurti Publications America

Illustrations, 288 pages, $14.95; ISBN: 1-884158-21-8

BICK PUBLISHING HOUSE
PRESENTS

Books on Wildlife Rehabilitation

by Dale Carlson and Irene Ruth
Step-by-Step Guides • Illustrated
Quick Reference for Wildlife Care
For parents, teachers, librarians who want
to learn and teach basic rehabilitation

Wildlife Care For Birds And Mammals
7-Volume Compendium
ISBN: 1-884158-16-1, $59.70

INCLUDES:
I Found A Baby Bird, What Do I Do?
I Found A Baby Duck, What Do I Do?
I Found A Baby Opossum, What Do I Do?
I Found A Baby Rabbit, What Do I Do?
I Found A Baby Raccoon, What Do I Do?
I Found A Baby Squirrel, What Do I Do?
First Aid For Wildlife

First Aid For Wildlife
ISBN: 1-884158-14-5, $9.95
Also available separately.

*Endorsed by Veterinarians, Wildlife Rehabilitation
Centers, and National Wildlife Magazines.*

ORDER FORM

16 MARION ROAD, BRANFORD, CT 06405
TEL/FAX 203-208-5253
www.bickpubhouse.com

Name: _____

Address: _____

City: _____ State: _____ Zip: _____

Phone: _____ Fax: _____

QTY	BOOK TITLE	PRICE	TOTAL
	YOUNG ADULT FICTION		
	The Human Apes	14.95	
	The Mountain of Truth	14.95	
	YOUNG ADULT NONFICTION		
	New! Out of Order	14.95	
	Understand Your Self	14.95	
	Addiction: The Brain Disease	14.95	
	Are You Human or What?	14.95	
	Cosmic Calendar: From the Big Bang to Your Consciousness	14.95	
	Girls Are Equal Too: The Teenage Girl's How-To-Survive Book	14.95	
	In and Out of Your Mind: Teen Science: Human Bites	14.95	
	Relationships: To Oneself, To Others, To the World	14.95	
	Stop the Pain: Teen Meditations	14.95	
	Talk: Teen Art of Communication	14.95	
	The Teen Brain Book: Who and What Are You?	14.95	
	What Are You Doing with Your Life?	14.95	
	Where's Your Head?: Psychology for Teenagers	14.95	
	Who Said What? Philosophy Quotes for Teens	14.95	
	ADULT HEALTH, RECOVERY & MEDITATION		
	Confessions of a Brain-Impaired Writer	14.95	
	The Courage to Lead: Mental Illnesses & Addictions	14.95	
	Stop the Pain: Adult Meditations	14.95	
	BOOKS ON LIVING WITH DISABILITIES		
	Living with Disabilities	59.70	
	BOOKS ON WILDLIFE REHABILITATION		
	First Aid for Wildlife	9.95	
	Wildlife Care for Birds and Mammals	59.70	
	TOTAL		
	SHIPPING & HANDLING: $4.00 (1 Book), $6.00 (2), $8.00 (3-10)		
	AMOUNT ENCLOSED		

Send check or money order to Bick Publishing House. Include shipping and handling.
**Also Available at your local bookstore from: Amazon.com, AtlasBooks, Baker & Taylor
Book Company, Follett Library Resources, and Ingram Book Company.**

AUTHOR
Dale Carlson

Author of over 70 books, adult and juvenile, fiction and nonfiction, Carlson has received three ALA Notable Book Awards, the Christopher Award, four *ForeWord* Book of the Year Awards, YALSA Best Picks for Young Adults, three New York Public Library Best Books for Teens, VOYA Honor Book. She writes science, psychology, dialogue and meditation books for young adults, and general adult nonfiction. Among her titles are *The Mountain of Truth* (ALA Notable Book), *Girls Are Equal Too* (ALA Notable Book), *Where's Your Head?: Psychology for Teenagers* (Christopher Award, New York Public Library Best Books List), *Stop the Pain: Teen Meditations* (New York Public Library Best Books List), *In and Out of Your Mind: Teen Science* (International Book of the Month Club, New York Public Library Best Books List), *Talk: Teen Art of Communication, Wildlife Care for Birds and Mammals, Stop the Pain: Adult Meditations.*

Recent Awarded books include *The Teen Brain Book: Who and What Are You?, In and Out of Your Mind, Teen Science: Human Bites, Talk: Teen Art of Communication, Are You Human Or What?, Addiction: The Brain Disease,* and *Understand Your Self.*

Carlson has lived and taught in the Far East: India, Indonesia, China, Japan. She teaches writing here and abroad during part of each year.

CO-AUTHOR
Michael Bower, Ed.D.

Dr. Michael Bower received undergraduate and master's degrees from Tufts University, a doctorate from Boston University and a Certificate of Advanced Studies from Harvard University. Dr. Bower has divided his career between education and counseling. He has been a school counselor, a director of a "school within a school" for special needs students, director of a school counseling program and a high school principal. He has taught graduate courses at Leslie University and Boston University. Recently, he was an assistant clinical professor in the Department of Psychiatry at the School of Medicine in Yale University. Dr. Bower had a private psychologist practice in Massachusetts and is currently a counselor at The Center for Change in New Haven, CT.

ILLUSTRATOR
Carol Nicklaus

Known as a character illustrator, her work has been featured in *The New York Times*, *Publishers Weekly*, *Good Housekeeping*, and *Mademoiselle*. To date she has done 150 books for Random House, Golden Press, Atheneum, Dutton, Scholastic, and Bick Publishing House. She has won awards from ALA, the Christophers, and The American Institute of Graphic Arts.